Just Listen 'n Learn
SPANISH

Sandra Truscott
José G. Escribano

D0377318

General editor, Brian Hill

Series advisers

Janet Jenkins
Duncan Sidwell
Al Wolff

PASSPORT BOOKS

Trade Imprint of National Textbook Company
Lincolnwood, Illinois U.S.A.

Acknowledgements

The Publishers and Dr Sandra Truscott would like to express their sorrow at the death of José Escribano during the preparation of this course.

Our thanks to Lourdes Litago and Fernando Olmedo for checking the manuscript.
Our thanks also to:
All the Spanish people who helped with the recordings in Spain and the Polytechnic of Central London for all studio recordings.

We are grateful to the following for permission to reproduce copyright material.

The Spanish Tourist Office for photographs on pages 54, 66, 89, 133, 150, 173, 215
Mary Glasgow Publications Ltd for the photographs on pages 78, 79, 95, 103, 124, 144, 187
Harrap Ltd for the photograph on page 167 and for the map on page 163
Derrick Croxon for the photographs on pages 32, 39, 47, 52, 53, 69, 111, 117, 121, 125, 175
Rosemary Senior for the photograph on page 137

Tape production: Gerald Ramshaw
Acting: Eloisa Fernandez, Miguel Peñaranda, Isabel Soto
Book design: Gillian Riley
Illustrations: Rowan Barnes-Murphy

1987 Printing

67890ML98

Contents

How to use this course

Following this course will help you understand, speak and read most of the Spanish you are likely to need on holiday or on business trips. The course is based on recordings made in Spain of ordinary Spanish people in everyday situations. Step by step you will learn first to understand what they are saying and then to speak in similar situations yourself.

Before producing the course we talked to literally hundreds of people about why and how they learn languages. We know how important it is for learning to be enjoyable – and for it to be usable as soon as possible. Again and again people told us that there was not much point in knowing all the grammar if you were unable to ask for a cup of coffee! In this course the only explanations of grammar will be ones that actually help you understand and use the language.

General hints to help you use the course

- Have confidence in us! Real language is complex and you will find certain things in every unit which are not explained in detail. Don't worry about this. We will build up your knowledge slowly, selecting only what is most important to know at each stage.
- Try to study regularly, but in short periods. 20–30 minutes each day is usually better than 3½ hours once a week.
- To help you learn to speak, say the words and phrases out loud whenever possible.
- If you don't understand something, leave it for a while. Learning a language is a bit like doing a jigsaw or a crossword: there are many ways to tackle it and it all falls into place eventually.
- Don't be afraid to write in the book and add your own notes.
- Do review frequently. (There are revision/review sections after every five units.) It helps to get somebody to test you – and they don't need to know Spanish.
- If you can possibly learn with somebody else you will be able to help each other and practise the language together.
- Learning Spanish may take more time than you thought. Just be patient and above all don't get angry with yourself.

Suggested study pattern

Each unit of the course consists of approximately fourteen pages in the book and ten minutes of tape. The first page of each unit will tell you what you are going to learn and suggest the best method of going about it. As you progress with the course you may find that you evolve a method of study which suits you better – that's fine, but we suggest you keep to our pattern at least for the first two or three units or you may find you are not taking full advantage of all the possibilities offered by the material.

The book contains step-by-step instructions for working through the course: when to use the book on its own, when to use the tape on its own, when to use them both together, and how to use them. On the tape the presenter will guide you through the various sections. Here is an outline of the study pattern proposed.

Dialogues   Listen to the dialogues, first without stopping the tape, and get a feel for the task ahead. Then go over each one bit by bit in conjunction with the vocabulary and the notes. You should get into the habit of using the PAUSE/STOP and REWIND buttons on your cassette recorder to give yourself time to think, to listen to sentences a number of times, and repeat them after the speakers. Don't leave a dialogue until you are confident that you have at least understood it.

(Symbols used in the notes are explained on p. 6.)

Key words and phrases	Study this list of the most important words and phrases from the dialogues. If possible, try to learn them by heart. They will be practised in the rest of the unit.
Practice what you have learned	This section contains a selection of exercises which focus your attention on the most important language in the unit. To do them you will need to work closely with the book and often your tape recorder – sometimes you are asked to write an exercise and then check the answers on the tape: other times to listen first and then fill in answers in the book. Again, use your PAUSE/STOP and REWIND buttons to give yourself time to think and to answer questions.
Grammar	At this stage in a unit things should begin to fall into place and you are ready for the grammar section. If you really don't like grammar, you will still learn a lot without studying this part, but most people quite enjoy finding out how the language they are using actually works and how it is put together. In each unit we have selected just one or two important grammar points.
Read and understand and *Did you know?*	In these sections you will be encouraged to read the kinds of signs, menus, brochures and so on you may come across in Spain and you will be given some practical background information on Spanish customs and culture.
Your turn to speak	Finally, back to the tape for some practise in speaking the main words and phrases which you have already heard and had explained. The book only gives you an outline of the exercises, so you are just listening to the tape and responding. Usually you will be asked to take part in a conversation where you hear a question or statement in Spanish, followed by a suggestion in English as to how you might reply. You then give your reply in Spanish and listen to see if you were right. You will probably have to go over these spoken exercises a few times before you get them absolutely correct.
Answers	The answers to all the exercises (except those given on tape) can be found on the last page of each unit.
	If you haven't learned languages using a tape before, just spend five minutes on Unit 1 getting used to the mechanics: practise pausing the tape, and see how long the rewind button needs to be pressed to recap on differing length phrases and sections.
	Don't be shy – take every opportunity you can to speak Spanish to Spanish people and to listen to real Spanish. Try listening to Spanish broadcasts on the radio. **¡Suerte!**

At the back of the book

At the back of the book is a reference section which contains:

Symbols and abbreviations

Spoken and written Spanish

Many of the conversations in this course were recorded in Andalusia in southern Spain which has an accent all of its own, though similar to the accent used in many parts of Southern America. The interesting point about this accent is that the s's on the ends of words tend to be dropped or swallowed in speech. Where this has occurred in a dialogue, we have shown it in the transcript by bracketing the s. For example, in dialogue 1 of Unit 3 María actually says ¿**cuánto dormitorio?** but the transcript reads ¿**cuánto(s) dormitorio(s)?**. Travelling around Spain you will come across many local accents, just as a Spaniard would travelling around the U.S. And if you are heading to any of the tourist resorts in southern Spain, this is the accent you will have to cope with every day!
As these dialogues were recorded 'live' you may hear the speakers hesitating or changing their minds as they talk. These 'false starts' are shown in brackets.

So much for the spoken Spanish in the course. Written Spanish has one or two peculiarities which you will no doubt notice a couple of pages into the book: firstly accents. These are used to emphasize a particular syllable or to differentiate in meaning between two words that are otherwise spelled the same e.g. **sí** yes, and **si** if. Secondly, upside down exclamation and question marks: these are advance warnings that the sentence coming up should be intonated differently.

1 Talking about yourself

What you will learn

- understanding and answering simple questions about yourself
- understanding and answering simple questions about your job
- asking others simple questions
- exchanging greetings
- addressing people in Spain

Before you begin

The introduction to the course on pp. 4–6 has some useful advice on studying alone and details the specific study pattern recommended for this particular course.

Look at the *Study guide* below. It has been designed to help you make the most effective use of the unit, so that you will go on from understanding the gist of the recorded dialogues to understanding them in detail and finally to being able to produce a number of key words, phrases and sentences yourself.

We shall be trying to develop your ability to *follow the gist* of spoken Spanish right from the start. So begin by listening to the first group of dialogues on the tape without using your book and without worrying about the details of what is being said.

Study guide

Use the study guide below to guide you through this unit. You may find it helpful to tick off each stage as you complete it.

	Dialogues 1 – 4: listen straight through, without the book
	Dialogues 1 – 4: listen, read and study one by one
	Dialogues 5 – 8: listen straight through, without the book
	Dialogues 5 – 8: listen, read and study one by one
	Dialogues 9 – 10: listen straight through, without the book
	Dialogues 9 – 10: listen, read and study one by one
	Study the *Key words and phrases*
	Do the exercises in *Practice what you have learned*
	Study the *Grammar* section and do the exercise
	Complete *Read and understand*
	Read *Did you know?*
	Do the tape exercise in *Your turn to speak*
	Finally, listen to all the dialogues again straight through

Dialogues

If you have a cassette recorder with a counter, put it to zero and note the counter reading for each dialogue in the square. This will help you find the dialogues more quickly when you want to listen to them a second time.
  Now turn on your tape recorder and start listening.

1 *Miguel tells us where he's from*

Pepe	Hola.
Miguel	Hola.
Pepe	¿Eres de Sevilla?
Miguel	Sí, soy sevillano.
Pepe	¿Eres español?
Miguel	Sí, soy español.

◆ **hola** hallo
◆ **sí** yes
  español Spanish

2 *Where are you from?*

Pepe	Hola.
Alejandro	Hola.
Pepe	¿Eres sevillano?
Alejandro	No, valenciano.
Pepe	¿Eres de Valencia?
Alejandro	Sí.
Pepe	¿De la ciudad de Valencia?
Alejandro	Sí.

◆ **no** no
  valenciano Valencian (from Valencia)

3 *John is a Canadian*

John	Soy canadiense, de Montreal.
Pepe	Bien, muchas gracias.
John	Vale.

  canadiense Canadian
◆ **bien** good, well, fine
◆ **muchas gracias** thanks very much
  vale OK

The most important expressions are marked with a ◗: these are the ones you should try to remember. They will be listed again on p. 14.

1 ◗ **¿eres de Sevilla?** are you from Seville? Notice that written Spanish has an upside down question mark ¿ at the beginning of the question. Spaniards indicate that they are asking a question by their intonation – listen carefully to the way Pepe asks:
¿eres de Sevilla? are you from Seville?
Without that intonation, Pepe would be making a statement:
eres de Sevilla you are from Seville

◗ **soy sevillano** I'm a Sevillian. Because the words 'I' and 'you' and 'he' are normally included in the verb in Spanish, you don't have to say them. **Soy sevillano** means 'I'm a Sevillian', **eres sevillano** means 'you are a Sevillian'. The verb 'to be' is on p. 17.

The difference between **sevillano** and **de Sevilla** is the same as that between **Londoner** and **from London**. **Sevillano** means 'a Sevillian' and **de Sevilla** 'from Seville'. There is another example of this in dialogue 2 with **valenciano** 'Valencian' and **de Valencia** 'from Valencia'.

2 **de la ciudad de Valencia** from the city of Valencia. Spanish nouns are divided into two groups called feminine and masculine (see p. 17 for further information). **La** is one of two words in Spanish meaning 'the' and it goes with 'feminine' words – **la ciudad** is one. You can often tell feminine words by their ending –a e.g. **la mesa** (table) or **la carta** (letter); unfortunately there are others that end in different ways, so you will have to learn them. In the vocabulary lists at the end of each dialogue, feminine words have been indicated by **la**. The masculine word for 'the' is **el** and lots of masculine words end in –o e.g. **el libro** (book) or **el tiempo** (weather).

3 **vale** OK. Mostly used by young people amongst friends; it might well be considered impolite if you were to use it to an older person. You will hear it used frequently in some areas of Spain – for instance the north – but not in others. You would do well to learn these expressions:
◗ **de acuerdo; está bien** both of which mean fine.

4 *Angeles and Marcos tell us where they are from*

Pepe	Y tú, ¿de dónde eres?
Angeles	De Sevilla.
Pepe	Y usted ¿de dónde es?
Marcos	De Corella, provincia de Navarra.

(la) **provincia** province

5 *Sandra talks about her job*

Americana	¿Eres estudiante?
Sandra	No, soy azafata.
Americana	¿Trabajas con Iberia?
Sandra	No, trabajo con British Airways.

♦ **con** with

6 *Pedro asks Luisa about her job*

Pedro	Y tú, ¿qué eres?
Luisa	Yo soy profesora.
Pedro	¿De qué das clases?
Luisa	De inglés.

7 *Pepe asks Roger about his nationality and his job*

Pepe	¿Eres español?
Roger	No, soy francés.
Pepe	¿Y trabajas aquí?
Roger	Trabajo aquí, en Sevilla, sí.
Pepe	¿Qué eres?
Roger	Soy peluquero.
Pepe	Gracias.
Roger	De nada.

francés French
♦ **aquí** here

4 ♦ **y tú ¿de dónde eres? y usted, ¿de dónde es?** both these phrases mean 'and where are you from?' (literally, 'and you, from where are you?'). Note that when Pepe talks to little Angeles he says **tu eres** – and when he talks to Marco, he uses **usted es**. This is because Spanish has two words for 'you'. **Usted** (often abbreviated in the written form to **Vd.** or **Ud.**) is formal and used between people who don't know each other well or as a sign of respect towards an older person. **Tú** is used between friends and when talking to children. As explained above you don't usually need to say the words for I, you etc. However, **usted** tends to be used because it is more polite. Note that the word for 'are' changes according to whether you use **tú** or **usted**, the familiar or the polite form.

♦ **¿es usted inglés?** are you English?
¿eres de Sevilla? are you from Seville?

5 ♦ **¿eres estudiante?** are you a student? Note that you don't need the word 'an' or 'a' in Spanish when you're talking about your profession. **¿eres médico?** are you a doctor?

♦ **soy azafata** I'm an air hostess. **Azafata** is an example of a feminine word ending in **a**. The word for a 'steward' is **camarero** and as another of its meanings is 'waiter', you should try to learn it. Why don't you look up the word for your own job in the dictionary? Or perhaps you're retired **jubilado** (man), **jubilada** (woman).

¿trabajas con Iberia? do you work with Iberia (airlines)?

♦ **trabajo con British Airways** I work with British Airways. Verbs in Spanish are classified into three groups. **Trabajar** (to work) is an **-ar** verb (see p. 17). Note the difference between I work (**trabajo**) and he works (**trabaja**). As in English, verb endings change according to *who* is performing the action. The endings for **-ar** verbs can be found on p. 17.

6 ♦ **soy profesora** I'm a teacher (Luisa talking.) If it were Pedro (a man) he would say **soy profesor**. Also note **español** (Spanish man), **española** (Spanish woman); **inglés** (English man), **inglesa** (English woman); **sevillano**, **sevillana** (Sevillian).

¿de qué das clases? what do you teach? (literally, 'of what do you give classes?') **dar** (to give) is another example of an **-ar** verb, although it is not regular.

7 ♦ **en Sevilla** in Seville. Other examples: **en Madrid, en Brighton, en Londres** (London).

♦ **¿qué eres?** what do you do? (literally, 'what are you?').

♦ **soy peluquero** I'm a hairdresser (Roger talking). If it were a woman talking, she would say **soy peluquera**.

♦ **de nada** you're welcome (lit. of nothing). Use this in reply to **gracias** (thanks) or **muchas gracias** (many thanks). You'll hear this a great deal in Spain.

	8	*María Teresa tells us something about herself*

Rosarito ¿Nombre, por favor?
María Teresa Mi nombre, María Teresa.
Rosarito ¿Señora o señorita?
María Teresa Señorita, a la fuerza.
Rosarito ¿Nacionalidad?
María Teresa Uy, española, ¡contentísima!

por favor please
mi my
a la fuerza not by choice
(la) nacionalidad nationality

	9	*Introducing friends*

Luisa Hola, Pepe, ¿qué tal? Pedro, éste es Pepe. Pepe, Pedro.
Pedro Hola, ¿ qué tal?
Pepe Muy bien. Encantado.
Pedro Tanto gusto.
Pepe El gusto es mío.

éste this
♦ **muy bien** very well

	10	*What languages do you speak?*

Pepe ¿Hablas francés?
Alejandro No sé.
Pepe ¿Y hablas inglés?
Alejandro No, tampoco.
Pepe ¿Qué hablas?
Alejandro Español.
Pepe ¿Y hablas valenciano?
Alejandro Sí.
♦ **no sé** I don't know
tampoco neither

8 ¿**nombre, por favor?** name please? This is what you will be asked on checking in at the hotel reception, i.e. it's the official way of asking someone their name; simply reply **Bill Smith** or **soy Bill Smith** = I'm Bill Smith.

♦ ¿**señora o señorita?** Mrs or Miss? **Señor** is Mr, Sir. These words are abbreviated on envelopes to **Sr** (Mr), **Sra** (Mrs) and **Srta** (Miss). There is no word for 'master' or 'Ms'!

uy, española, ¡contentísima! hey, Spanish, and proud of it! Like question marks, exclamation marks are also used at the beginning as well as the end of an exclamation. But upside down too!

9 ♦ ¿**qué tal?** how are you? (used with friends).

♦ **éste es Pepe** this is Pepe. A simple but polite way of introducing someone. This dialogue contains a number of set phrases used in introductions. We suggest you learn just one as they all mean much the same, e.g. **encantado** = delighted (to meet you); **tanto gusto** = pleased to meet you (literally much pleasure); **el gusto es mío** = the pleasure is mine. Of course, you may *hear* any of them.

10 ♦ ¿**hablas francés?** do you speak French? **Hablar** (to speak) is another example of an **-ar** verb. Pepe is talking to a child, so he uses the **tú** form (**tú**) ¿**hablas?** If he were talking to an adult he would use (**usted**) ¿**habla?** In reply, you should say **sí, hablo francés** 'yes, I speak French' or **no, hablo inglés** 'no, I speak English'.

Key words and phrases

Here are some key words and phrases that you should learn by heart. They'll be practised thoroughly in the exercises which follow. As you see, they deal in the main with introductions and information about where people are from, what they do, the languages they speak and where they work.

¡hola!	hello!
¿qué tal?	how are you?
soy (Bill Smith)	I'm (Bill Smith)
éste es (John)	this is (John)
encantado	delighted to meet you
¿de dónde es usted?	where are you from?
¿es usted . . .	are you . . .
de (Torremolinos)?	from (Torremolinos)?
español/española?	Spanish?
estudiante?	a student?
¿qué es usted?	what are you?/what do you do?
soy . . .	I'm . . .
de (Bath)	from Bath
inglés/inglesa	English
peluquero/peluquera	a hairdresser
camarero	a waiter/a steward
trabajo . . .	I work . . .
con (British Airways)	with (British Airways)
en (Londres)	in (London)
¿habla usted (inglés)?	do you speak (English)?
hablo (inglés)	I speak (English)

Also note these important words and expressions:

sí yes
no no
y and
con with
¿dónde? where
de acuerdo } fine
está bien }
(muchas) gracias thank you (very much)
de nada you're welcome
bien good, fine
muy bien very good
por favor please
aquí here
no sé I don't know

Practice what you have learned

The following exercises will help you to listen accurately and to understand the language in the dialogues more fully. You'll need both the book and the tape: later, you will be able to practise speaking with the use of your cassette player alone.

Don't start until you have read and understood the instructions at the beginning of each exercise. You may be asked to read the text, to write down answers or to listen to the tape. Sometimes you will have to stop your recorder in order to give yourself time to think. Answers which don't appear on tape will be found at the end of the unit, on p. 20.

1 Ana has interviewed Jaime for a survey but unfortunately the printing department has mixed up their conversation. Can you sort out the correct order for the sentences below? When you have completed the exercise, listen to the tape where you will hear the dialogue in the correct order.

Ana ¿Es usted español?   *Ana* ....

Jaime Vale.   *Jaime* ....

Ana Hola.   *Ana* ....

Ana Muchas gracias.   *Jaime* ....

Jaime No, soy americano.   *Ana* ....

Jamie Hola.   *Jaime* ....

2 A customs officer (**un aduanero**) is interviewing two people at the airport in Madrid. From the information supplied, work out how they would answer the following questions. First, fill in their replies, then listen to the cassette where you will hear the full dialogue.

José García: a Spaniard, teacher of French and English, from Madrid
Ruth Sadler: José's fiancée, English, hairdresser, from London, works in Madrid

The customs officer interviews José first.

Aduanera ¿Nombre, por favor?   *Aduanero* ¿Nacionalidad?

José ....   *Ruth* ....

Aduanera ¿Qué es usted?   *Aduanero* ¿Nombre, por favor?

José ....   *Ruth* ....

Aduanera ¿Habla inglés?   *Aduanero* ¿Señora o señorita?

José ....   *Ruth* ....

Aduanera ¿Habla francés?   *Aduanero* ¿Qué es usted?

José ....   *Ruth* ....

Aduanera ¿Nacionalidad?   *Aduanero* ¿De dónde es?

José ....   *Ruth* ....

Aduanera ¿De dónde es usted?   *Aduanero* ¿Trabaja aquí?

José ....   *Ruth* ....

3 Here are four people – ask them what they do for a living by using the phrase ¿es usted . . . . . ? and then write in the question beneath the appropriate illustration. (The first one has been done for you.) When you have filled in the gaps, listen to your cassette where you will hear both the questions and the answers.

a ¿es usted b .... c .... d ....
profesor? ....

4 For this exercise you must listen to the tape *first*, where you will hear descriptions of four different people. Listen to the tape several times to ensure you understand it before inserting ✓ in the boxes according to whether the statements are true **verdad** or false **mentira**. The answers to this exercise are on page 20. You will hear a new word: **pero** but.

a. Pepe is from Valencia   verdad ☐   mentira ☐

b. María is Spanish   verdad ☐   mentira ☐

c. She's from Valencia too   verdad ☐   mentira ☐

d. Cristina is a hairdresser   verdad ☐   mentira ☐

e. She is from Valencia   verdad ☐   mentira ☐

f. John is from Birmingham   verdad ☐   mentira ☐

g. He is a hairdresser   verdad ☐   mentira ☐

h. He works in Manchester   verdad ☐   mentira ☐

5 Listen to your cassette again where you'll hear six people telling you where they are from. Can you insert the information they give you below? You may have to listen to the tape more than once.

a. .... Miguel ....

b. .... Laura ....

c. .... John ....

d. .... Isabel ....

e. .... Roger ....

f. .... Sandra ....

Now rewind your tape again and listen to the correct replies.

Grammar

The verb 'to be' is very important in Spanish so the grammar section in this first unit begins with its present tense. As you have learnt, you don't have to use words for 'I', 'you' etc in Spanish. They are given in this first unit, but they won't be included with verbs later. You'll also find that all the translations are included in this unit, although these too will be omitted in later units. If you find you can't remember what a particular verb form means, simply check back to this unit.

Ser to be

yo soy	I am	**nosotros somos**	we are
tú eres	you are (informal)	**vosotros sois**	you are (informal plural)
él es	he is	**ustedes son**	you are (formal plural)
ella es	she is	**ellos son**	they are (men or men *and* women)
		ellas son	they are (women)

Use **ser**
.a. when you're talking about professions: **soy ingeniero** I'm an engineer
b. when you're saying who you are: **soy María** I'm Maria
c. when you're saying where you're from: **soy francés** I'm French; **soy de Londres** I'm from London

-ar endings

There are three groups of verbs in Spanish: verbs with **-ar** endings (**fum<u>ar</u>** = to smoke), verbs with **-er** endings (**com<u>er</u>** = to eat), and verbs with **-ir** endings (**dorm<u>ir</u>** = to sleep). Most **-ar** verbs have the same endings in the present tense, so do try and learn them. And remember, you don't need to use the pronoun in Spanish as the endings 'represent' the pronouns. For instance, **-mos** is the ending for the pronoun 'we': **fumamos** = we smoke, **comimos** = we eat, **dormimos** = we sleep.

It will probably seem awkward and difficult at first that there are so many endings, but don't worry as you will very soon learn to recognize them. Note also that **ell<u>os</u>** is the normal word for 'they'. You only use **ell<u>as</u>** if all of 'them' are feminine e.g. if you are talking to a group of women.

hablar	to speak		
yo habl<u>o</u>	I speak	**nosotros habl<u>amos</u>**	we speak
tú habl<u>as</u>	you speak (informal)	**vosotros habl<u>áis</u>**	you speak (informal plural)
él habl<u>a</u>	he speaks		
ella habl<u>a</u>	she speaks	**ustedes habl<u>an</u>**	you speak (formal)
		ellos habl<u>an</u>	they speak
		ellas habl<u>an</u>	they speak

1 Here's another **-ar** verb: **estudiar** (to study). Can you write out its present tense? Answers on p. 20.

Genders

Spanish nouns (names of things) and adjectives (words which describe nouns) are either *masculine* or *feminine*. If the word is masculine then the word 'the' which accompanies it is **el**. If the word is feminine, then 'the' is **la**.
el libro the book; **la mesa** the table
Also note that, as in the above examples, most masculine nouns end in an **o** and most feminine nouns in an **a**.

Words referring to men are always masculine and those referring to women are always feminine. How do you change a word like **sevillano** into the feminine form?

a. if the word ends in an **o**, simply substitute that final **o** with an **a**
   el sevillano the Sevillian (man)
   la sevillana the Sevillian (woman)

b. if the word ends in a consonant, add an **a**
   el profesor the (male) teacher   **el inglés** the Englishman
   la profesora the (female) teacher   **la inglesa** the Englishwoman

c. if the word ends in an **e**, it remains the same for both masculine and feminine forms
   el canadiense the Canadian (man)
   la canadiense the Canadian (woman)

Read and understand

This short passage uses some of the language you have learnt in this first unit. See if you can understand it.

Pepe es de Sevilla, es sevillano. Trabaja en Valencia, es profesor de inglés y habla francés y valenciano también. Juanita es de Corella. Es azafata y trabaja con Iberia. Habla francés y español. Teresa es estudiante de inglés.

And now can you answer these questions in English? Answers on p. 20.

a. Where is Juanita from? ....

b. What languages does she speak? ....

c. What does she do for a living? ....

d. Where does Pepe work? ....

e. What does he do? ....

f. What language is Teresa studying? ....

Did you know?

Señor

Spaniards use **señor**, **señora** and **señorita** rather more than we use their equivalents in English. They are used with the family names – señor Escribano, señora García – and by themselves to attract someone's attention. ¡**Señor, aquí!** (Over here sir!). **Buenos días, señora** (Good morning, Madam).

Don

You may also come across the use of **don** and **doña** (abbreviated on envelopes and signs as D and Dña) as in don Juan! It is used as a token of respect for the elderly and respected members of the community. At work, especially when talking to an employer, you have to use it. It is used with the christian name – don Carlos, doña María – or in front of the whole name – don Serafín Cuesta Calvo. Sometimes, as in the case of addresses on envelopes you write **señor**, **señora** or **señorita** (abbreviated) before **don** or **doña**. For example, **Sr. D. Serafín Cuesta Calvo**.

Apellidos (family names)

It may surprise you at first that Spaniards have two family names – **José G. Escribano Pérez** is not Mr Perez, but Mr Escribano Pérez, or Mr Escribano. The reason for the two family names is that a Spanish woman keeps her maiden name on marriage and therefore children receive the first family name of each one of their parents, although frequently they will only use their father's.

Señora de . . .

Although officially and legally Spanish women keep their maiden names, 'socially' they are often referred to by their husband's family name preceded by **de** (of), **Señora de Sánchez** or **María Gómez de Sánchez**. The same applies for **Señores de Cuesta** (Mr and Mrs Cuesta).

Gracias

Don't be surprised if you don't hear **gracias** or **muchas gracias** as frequently as you would like – Spaniards don't pepper their conversation with 'thanks' or 'thank you very much' as frequently as the English but that doesn't mean they are any less polite.

Your turn to speak

Now you are going to practise speaking some of the language you have learned in the dialogues. Once you have read the instructions to the exercise, turn on the tape and try not to look at the book – unless you want to check a point. You will be taking part in some conversations and answering questions in Spanish. Isabel will tell you what to say, in English. After her prompt, stop the tape and say the phrase out loud in Spanish. Then start the tape again and you'll hear what you should have said. It may take you some time to work out how to do this type of exercise, but we'll be using this technique throughout the course, so you'll soon get used to it.

For this exercise, imagine you're a woman. You're in a Spanish bar, see how well you can talk to the man at the table next to yours. You will be practising:

Greetings
Soy (Anne)
Trabajo en (Madrid)
Soy (inglés/inglesa)
Soy (peluquera/azafata)
Trabajo con (Iberia/British Airways)

And finally   Don't forget to play through all the dialogues again without looking at your book.

Answers

Practice what you have learned p. 16 Exercise **4** (**a**) mentira (**b**) verdad (**c**) mentira (**d**) mentira (**e**) verdad (**f**) verdad (**g**) verdad (**h**) verdad.

Grammar p. 17 Exercise **1** estudio, estudias, estudia, estudiamos, estudiáis, estudian.

Read and understand p. 18 (**a**) from Corella (**b**) French and Spanish (**c**) she's an air hostess (**d**) Valencia (**e**) he's a teacher of English (**f**) English.

2 Yourself and others

What you will learn

- understanding and answering questions about yourself
- understanding and answering questions about your family
- asking similar questions of others
- saying if you are married or single
- counting from one to ten
- something about the regions of Spain

Before you begin

The study guide set out below is very similar to the one in Unit 1.
Remember that the first stage of listening to the dialogues straight through
is important even if you do not understand much of what is being said. A
great deal of success in language learning depends on being able to pick out
the words you know from a torrent of words you don't and then making
some intelligent guesses.

Study guide

As in Unit 1, use the study pattern below to guide you through this unit.
You may find it helpful to tick off each stage as you complete it.

	Dialogues 1 – 4: listen straight through, without the book
	Dialogues 1 – 4: listen, read and study one by one
	Dialogues 5 – 7: listen straight through, without the book
	Dialogues 5 – 7: listen, read and study one by one
	Study the *Key words and phrases*
	Do the exercises in *Practice what you have learned*
	Study the *Grammar* section
	Complete *Read and understand*
	Read *Did you know?*
	Do the tape exercises in *Your turn to speak*
	Finally, listen to all the dialogues again straight through

Dialogues

1 *A geography test*

Pepe	Hola.
Miriam	Hola.
Pepe	¿Cómo te llamas?
Miriam	Miriam.
Pepe	¿Eres de Barcelona o de Madrid?
Miriam	De Sevilla. Soy de Sevilla.
Pepe	¿Dónde está Sevilla?
Miriam	En el sur.
Pepe	¿Y Barcelona?
Miriam	Barcelona está en el norte.
Pepe	¿Dónde está Valencia?
Miriam	Valencia está en el este de España.
Pepe	¿Y dónde está Portugal?
Miriam	Portugal está en el oeste de España.

(el) sur south
(el) norte north
(el) este east
(el) oeste west

2 *Are you married or single?*

Pepe	Hola Pablo.
Pablo	Hola.
Pepe	¿Estás casado?
Pablo	No.
Pepe	¿Tienes novia?
Pablo	No.
Pepe	¿No?
Pablo	No.
Pepe	¿De verdad?
Pablo	De verdad.

¿de verdad? really?

1 ¿cómo te llamas? what are you called?/what's your name? (lit. how do you call yourself?) You will probably hear the polite form ¿cómo se llama usted? more frequently, to which you should reply me llamo Bill Smith. You can also answer by simply giving your name.

♦ ¿dónde está Sevilla? where is Seville? Note that here Pepe uses a different verb for 'to be' estar. Both ser (which you have already learnt) and estar mean the same but are used in different situations (more about this in *Grammar* p. 31). For the moment, make a mental note whenever estar is used in the dialogues.

2 ♦ ¿estás casado? are you married?

♦ ¿tienes novia? have you got a girlfriend? Tener (to have) is the first example of an -er verb. Tener is an irregular verb but one that you will have to use so often in conversation that you *must* learn its present tense by heart (see p. 31). Note also that you don't use una with novia just as in the question ¿eres azafata? = are you an air hostess? the una was omitted.

☐ **3** *Do you have a friend?*

Pepe   Hola, Miriam.
Miriam Hola.
Pepe   ¿Estás casada?
Miriam No.
Pepe   ¿Tienes novio?
Miriam No.
Pepe   ¿Tienes un amigo?
Miriam Sí.
Pepe   ¿Cómo se llama?
Miriam Juan.
Pepe   Gracias. Adiós.
Miriam Adiós.

    (el) amigo friend
♦ **adiós** goodbye

☐ **4** *Talking about your children*

Pepe ¿Está casada?
Neni Sí.
Pepe ¿Tiene hijos?
Neni Sí, dos.
Pepe ¿(Eh) son chicos o chicas?
Neni Chico y chica.
Pepe ¿Cuántos años tienen?
Neni El chico cinco, la chica dos.
Pepe Gracias.
Neni De nada.

♦ **dos** two
  (el) chico boy
  (la) chica girl
♦ **cinco** five

3 ¿estás casada? are you married? Earlier Pepe had asked Pablo ¿estás casad<u>o</u>? Here, because he is talking to a girl, Pepe must use the feminine form casad<u>a</u>.

♦ ¿tienes novio? have you got a boyfriend? Note these two words novi<u>o</u> 'boyfriend' and novi<u>a</u> 'girlfriend'.

♦ ¿cómo se llama? what is he called? (lit. how does he call himself?).

4 ♦ ¿está casada? are you married? Here Pepe is addressing Neni formally so he must use the usted form ¿está (usted) casada? As you have already learnt in Unit 1, there is no need in Spanish to translate the 'you'.

♦ ¿tiene hijos? do you have any children? Here again Pepe is using the formal form ¿tiene (usted) hijos? In the singular hijo means son, but in the plural hijos means 'children' as well as 'sons'. By the way, if you don't have any children, the answer would be no tengo hijos.

♦ ¿cuántos años tienen? how old are they? (lit. how many years have they?) Here is the verb tener (to have) in the plural. Spaniards express the idea of age, not by saying they *are* ten years old, but that they *have* ten years. tengo diez años I am (have) ten years old. So when Pepe asks how old Neni's children are, he has to say 'how many years have they?' and he has to use the word cuánto 'how much, how many?'. Because he is talking about years in the plural, he says cuántos
¿cuánto tiempo? how long, how much time?
¿cuántos años tiene? how old are you?

5 *Counting money*

Pepe	Dámaso, ¿cuánto dinero tienes?
Damaso	Tres.
Pepe	¿Tres qué?
Damaso	Tres pesetas.
Pepe	¿Y ahora cuánto dinero tienes?
Damaso	Cuatro.
Pepe	¿Cuatro pesetas?
Damaso	No, tres pesetas y un duro.

♦ **ahora** now
♦ **cuatro** four
un duro a five peseta coin

6 *Do you sell . . .?*

Pepe	Por favor, ¿venden ustedes cremas para la piel?
María	En la sección de perfumería.
Pepe	¿Dónde está?
María	En planta baja.
Pepe	¿En la planta baja?
María	Planta baja.
Pepe	¿Y dónde venden los juguetes para niños?
María	Eso está todo en la tercera planta.

la sección section
la perfumería cosmetics department
en la planta baja on the ground floor
el juguete toy
eso that
el niño boy, child
♦ **todo** everything
en la tercera planta on the third floor

7 *Can you speak more slowly?*

Ana	¿Cómo se llama usted?
Susan	No comprendo. Lo siento – despacio por favor.
Ana	Nombre . . .
Susan	¡Ah! Susan Brown . . .
Ana	¿Está usted casada?
Susan	No, no estoy casada. Soy soltera.

5   ¿**cuánto dinero tienes**? how much money do you have?

       tres pesetas three pesetas. This dialogue contains a number of plural nouns. You may have already worked out that to make a word which ends in a vowel plural, you usually add an **s**

peseta (peseta)	**chico** (boy)
pesetas (pesetas)	**chicos** (boys)

       If the word ends in a consonant you add **es**. For example, you have already learnt the word **ciudad** (city) – if you want to talk about 'cities', simply say **ciudades**.

    ◆ You will find all the numbers from 1 – 10 in *Key words and phrases* on p. 28.

6   ¿**venden ustedes cremas para la piel**? do you sell skin creams? **Vender** = to sell is a regular **-er** verb and its present tense can be found on p. 31.

7 ◆ **no comprendo** I don't understand. Vital for foreigners! As is the next phrase . . .

    ◆ **lo siento** I'm sorry (lit. I feel it). From the verb **sentir** = to feel.

    ◆ **despacio por favor** slowly please.

    ◆ **no estoy casada** I'm not married. Note the following
       estoy I am
       no estoy I am not
       comprendo I understand
       no comprendo I don't understand

    ◆ **soy soltera** I'm single. Also note these meanings: **soltero** = bachelor and **soltera** = unmarried woman.

Key words and phrases

Here are the most important words and phrases that you have met in this unit. Be sure you know them, and practise saying them aloud.

¿dónde está Sevilla?
¿cómo se llama usted?
me llamo . . .

where is Seville?
what's your name?
my name is . . .

no comprendo
¿cuántos años tiene?
tengo (diez) años

I don't understand
how old are you?
I'm (ten) years old

¿está casado/casada?
no – soy soltero/soltera

are you married?
no I'm single (no, I'm a bachelor/an unmarried woman)

sí – estoy casado/casada

yes – I'm married

¿tiene novio/novia?

do you have a boyfriend/girlfriend?

¿tiene hijos?
sí, tengo hijos
sí, tengo tres hijos

do you have any childen?
yes, I have children
yes, I have three children

lo siento
despacio, por favor

I'm sorry
slowly, please

adiós
ahora

goodbye
now

uno, dos, tres
cuatro, cinco, seis
siete, ocho, nueve
diez

one, two, three
four, five, six
seven, eight, nine
ten

Practice what you have learned

And now for some exercises where you will need to use both book and cassette. The exercises are designed to help you listen accurately and to understand the language in the dialogues more fully. Remember that you'll get a chance to speak yourself later.

Read the instructions in the book first as you will be doing different things in each exercise.

1 Listen to the cassette where you will hear a conversation similar to dialogue 1. Read the statements below and tick the appropriate box according to whether the statement is true **verdad** or false **mentira**. Listen for two new words: **también** (as well/also) and ¡**hombre**! (lit. man!) used frequently in Spanish to express surprise. Answers on p. 34.

a. San Sebastián está en el norte de España.
verdad ☐
mentira ☐

b. Huelva está en el sur de España.
verdad ☐
mentira ☐

c. Badajoz está en el sur.
verdad ☐
mentira ☐

d. Valencia está en el oeste de España.
verdad ☐
mentira ☐

e. Alonso no es español.
verdad ☐
mentira ☐

2 On tape you will hear four people talking about themselves. Listen carefully, as often as you need, then look at the illustrations below and insert the correct name against the corresponding picture and description. Their names are Julio, Juanito, Pili and Mari-Carmen. Answers on p. 34.

a. ....
sevillana, soltera, tiene novio

b. ....
casado, dos hijas, una de dos años, otra de cinco

c. ....
soltero, tiene amiga en Valencia

d. ....
de Corella, tiene novio de Corella

3 Listen to a short description of a Spanish department store **El Corte Inglés**. Fill in the items that are sold on each floor. You will learn two new words **pan** = bread and **planta sótano** = basement. Answers on p. 34.

```
┌─────────────────────────────────────────────┐
│                                               │
│          EL CORTE INGLES                      │
│                                               │
│           TERCERA PLANTA                      │
│                                               │
│   .........................................   │
│   .........................................   │
│                                               │
│             PLANTA BAJA                       │
│                                               │
│   .........................................   │
│   .........................................   │
│                                               │
│           PLANTA SOTANO                       │
│                                               │
│   .........................................   │
│   .........................................   │
│                                               │
└─────────────────────────────────────────────┘
```

4 On tape you will hear some numbers between one and ten. Write them down in figures. You can check your answers on p. 34.

a. ....

b. ....

c. ....

d. ....

e. ....

f. ....

Grammar

Vender to sell

vendo	I sell	**vendemos**	we sell
vendes	you sell (informal)	**vendéis**	you sell (informal)
vende	he/she sells	**venden**	they sell
vende	you sell (formal)	**venden**	you sell (formal)

Tener to have

tengo	I have	**tenemos**	we have
tienes	you have (informal)	**tenéis**	you have (informal)
tiene	he/she has	**tienen**	they have
tiene	you have (formal)	**tienen**	you have (formal)

Remember that as well as meaning 'to have' **tener** is also used in Spanish to say how old you are: **tengo diez años** I am ten years old.

Plurals of nouns

To form the plural of a noun add an **s** if the noun ends in a vowel

el amigo the friend	**los amigos** the friends
la novia the girlfriend	**las novias** the girlfriends

If it ends in a consonant add **es**

la ciudad the city	**las ciudades** the cities
el profesor the teacher	**los profesores** the teachers

If it ends in a **z** change the **z** to **c** and add **es**

una vez	one time	**unas veces**	some times
el lápiz	the pencil	**los lápices**	the pencils

Estar to be

In Spanish there are two verbs for 'to be' **ser** (see Unit 1) and **estar**. Here is the present tense of **estar**.

estoy	I am	**estamos**	we are
estás	you are	**estáis**	you are
está	you/he/she is	**están**	you/they are

Here are the rules that govern the use of **ser** and **estar**:
Ser is used to describe who you are: **soy Ana** I'm Anne
and what you are: **soy inglés** I'm English   **soy azafata** I'm an air-hostess
Estar is used to describe where people and things are:
¿dónde está Juan? where is Juan?   **¿dónde está la maleta?** where is the suitcase?
and to describe a temporary mood or reaction: **estoy contento** I'm happy
But note that when referring to marital status you say:
¿está casado/casada? are you married?   **soy soltero/soltera** I'm single

Read and understand

Here is a list of selected departments in **El Corte Inglés**. There are some new, but easy, vocabulary items – which are explained below.

EL CORTE INGLES	
tercera planta	sombreros, pantalones
segunda planta	pan, café, vino
primera planta	juguetes
planta baja	perfumería
planta sótano	servicios

(el) sombrero hat
(los) pantalones trousers
(el) café coffee
(el) vino wine
(los) servicios lavatories

Reply to the following statements with **sí** or **no**. (Answers p. 34.)

a. Los sombreros están en la planta baja ....
b. El vino está en la planta sótano ....
c. El café está en la planta baja ....
d. Los servicios están en la planta sótano ....
e. Los juguetes están en la planta baja ....

Did you know?

Covering some 300,000 sq. miles, Spain is the third largest European country. The Spanish flag also flies over the Balearic and Canary Islands and the provinces of Ceuta and Melilla on the African coast – though these are more like cities than provinces.

The physical characteristics of the country (one of the most mountainous in Europe) make for an uneven distribution of population. Valencia, Galicia, Catalonia and the Basque provinces are more densely peopled than the central plateau (Castile and Aragon) which suffers from a shortage of water. Neither Spain's people nor her scenery are cast in the same mould. Every place on the map has its own character and mood varying like the accents, the climates, the folklore and the language. You will be learning **castellano** (Castilian Spanish) in this course, the official language of Spain and the language used by more than three-quarters of the Spanish population. It is also the form of Spanish spoken in Mexico and Central and South America (with the exception of Brazil). However, alongside castilian, **catalán** is spoken in Catalonia (encompassing the provinces of Gerona, Barcelona, Tarragona and Lérida), and in the Cantabrian area both **vascuence** (Basque) and **gallego** (Galician) are spoken. **Vascuence** is thought to have been the original language of the Iberian Peninsula but it bears little resemblance to **castellano**, and **gallego** is said to sound more like Portuguese than Spanish!

Your turn to speak

1 Miguel will ask you some simple questions about yourself. You will answer some of them – such as your name – with English words. Miguel's fourth question will be ¿**tiene usted hermanos o hermanas**? (do you have any brothers or sisters?) to which you should reply **tengo**................ Don't worry about making mistakes; the important thing is for you to understand the questions and to make a reply of some kind. NB One of the questions concerns what you do for a living, try looking it up in a dictionary or better still ask a Spanish-speaking pérson.

2 You've just met a rather inquisitive Spanish man. Reply to his questions about your background – Isabel will prompt you on what to say. You will be practising: **soy de**, **estoy casado**.

3 You're shopping in a department store – ask one of the assistants where things are. You will be practising: ¿**dónde**? ¿**dónde está**? ¿**venden**?

Answers

Practice what you have learned p. 29 Exercise 1 (**a**) verdad (**b**) verdad (**c**) verdad (**d**) mentira (**e**) mentira

p. 29 Exercise 2 (**a**) Mari Carmen (**b**) Juanito (**c**) Julio (**d**) Pili

p. 30 Exercise 3 (**a**) la planta baja – sección de perfumería, cremas para la piel (**b**) la tercera planta – juguetes para niños (**c**) la planta sótano – pan

p. 30 Exercise 4 (**a**) 10 (**b**) 7 (**c**) 4 (**d**) 8 (**e**) 3 (**f**) 5

Read and understand p. 32 (**a**) no (**b**) no (**c**) no (**d**) sí (**e**) no.

3 Getting information

What you will learn

- asking questions
- booking in at hotels and campsites
- asking where things are
- using numbers up to 20
- something about Spanish hotels and campsites

Before you begin

Most conversations involve asking for and understanding information of one kind or another. With a foreign language it is important to develop the skill of listening for the *gist* of what someone is saying – all too often people panic because they don't understand every word when in fact they do understand as much as they need to for practical purposes.

Follow the study guide below to make sure you make the most effective use of the unit.

Study guide

	Dialogues 1 – 4: listen straight through, without the book
	Dialogues 1 – 4: listen, read and study one by one
	Dialogues 5 – 7: listen straight through, without the book
	Dialogues 5 – 7: listen, read and study one by one
	Study the *Key words and phrases*
	Do the exercises in *Practice what you have learned*
	Study the *Grammar* section and do the exercise
	Complete *Read and understand*
	Read *Did you know?*
	Do the tape exercise in *Your turn to speak*
	Finally, listen to all the dialogues again straight through

Dialogues

☐ **1** *Describing your home*

María ¿Vive en una casa o en un piso?
Pepe En una casa.
María ¿Cuánto(s) dormitorio(s) tiene su casa?
Pepe Tres, tres dormitorios.
María ¿Tiene un jardín grande?
Pepe (Eh) no muy grande, pero tiene un jardín.

(el) **jardín** garden
grande big

☐ **2** *Where are the lavatories?*

Pepe Por favor, ¿dónde están los servicios?
María Hay en toda(s) planta(s) meno(s) en la de abajo, la planta baja.
Pepe En todas las plantas hay.
María Meno(s) en la planta baja.
Pepe Meno(s) en la planta baja.
Pepe ¿Para señoras y para caballeros?
María Sí, ambo(s) sexo(s).
Pepe Ambos sexos. Gracias.

♦ **para** for
♦ (el) **caballero** gentleman
ambos sexos both sexes

☐ **3** *Is there a chemist/pharmacy nearby?*

Pepe ¿Hay una farmacia por aquí cerca?
Alejandro Sí, está al lado.
Pepe ¿A la derecha o a la izquierda?
Alejandro A la derecha.
Pepe Gracias.

al lado next door

1 ¿vive en una casa o en un piso? do you live in a house or a flat? **Vivir** = to live is an example of the third type of Spanish verb, those that end in **-ir**. The full form is given on p. 45. ¿**dónde vive/vives?** where do you live? is a phrase you will often be asked on holiday and you should both learn to recognize it and be able to answer

♦ **vivo en . . .** I live in . . . . or **vivo aquí** I live here.

¿**cuántos dormitorios tiene su casa?** how many bedrooms does your house have? **su** = your. **Cuántos dormitorios**: note how in this example the noun **dormitorios** and the adjective **cuántos** *agree*. **Dormitorio** is a masculine plural word and therefore **cuántos** must also be masculine and plural.

2 ♦ **por favor, ¿dónde están los servicios?** excuse me, where are the lavatories? And Maria replies
hay en todas las plantas there are (lavatories) on all floors;
hay can mean there is or there are
menos en la de abajo except on the ground floor.

3 ♦ ¿**hay una farmacia por aquí cerca?** is there a chemist's near here? This is a very useful sentence to know if you want to locate a particular place in the area. Just substitute the place you want **bar, café, banco** etc for **farmacia**. ¿**hay un bar por aquí?** is there a bar near here? ¿**hay un banco por aquí?** is there a bank near here?

♦ ¿**a la derecha o a la izquierda?** to the right or to the left? Learn these words well and you won't get lost on holiday! Also note: **al final de la calle** at the end of the street; **todo recto** straight on; **en el cruce** at the crossroads.

	4	*Describing what you see*

Pepe	¿Qué hay en la mesa?
Miguel	Una botella de vino.
Pepe	¿Y hay otra botella?
Miguel	Sí, una botella de Coca-Cola.
Pepe	¿(Una . . .) qué prefieres, vino o Coca-Cola?
Miguel	Coca-Cola.
Pepe	Bien. ¿Qué más hay en la mesa?
Miguel	Hay un reloj, vario(s) lápice(s) y cigarrillo(s).
Pepe	¿Y hay una caja de cerillas en la mesa?
Miguel	Sí, también.
Pepe	¿Dónde está?
Miguel	Al lado de la botella de Coca-Cola.

(el) lápiz pen
(el) cigarrillo cigarette
(la) caja box
(la) cerilla match

	5	*A double room for one night . . .*

Pepe	¿Tiene una habitación libre?
Receptionista	Sí ¿Cómo la prefiere, sencilla o de matrimonio?
Pepe	De matrimonio, por favor.
Receptionista	Lo siento, pero de matrimonio no tengo. Hay de dos camas.
Pepe	De dos camas . . ., bueno, bueno, vale, vale.
Receptionista	¿Para cuántas noches?
Pepe	Para una, solamente para una.
Receptionista	¿Cómo la prefiere, con ducha o sin ducha?
Pepe	¿Tiene con baño?
Receptionista	No.
Pepe	Bueno, pues entonces con ducha.

◗ **sencilla** single
◗ **de matrimonio** double
◗ **bueno** well
solamente only
(el) baño bath
(la) ducha shower
◗ **sin** without
entonces then

4 ◆ **¿qué hay en la mesa?** what's on the table?

una botella de vino a bottle of wine. Wine is usually **blanco** (white) or **tinto** (red). **Tinto**, however, can only be used to describe *red wine*. If you want to describe other red objects then use **rojo**; **un vestido rojo** – a red dress.

◆ **¿qué prefieres, vino o Coca-Cola?** which do you prefer, wine or Coca-Cola? You'll hear the more formal **¿qué prefiere (usted)?** when in restaurants and bars. **¿Qué prefiere agua mineral con gas o sin gas?** which do you prefer, carbonated or still water? **Preferir** is another -ir verb like **vivir** but it isn't regular. You'll find both these verbs in the grammar section.

¿qué más hay en la mesa? what else is there on the table? **Más** is usually translated as more.

5 ◆ **¿tiene una habitación libre?** do you have a room free? **Habitación** means both room and bedroom.

¿cómo la prefiere? what sort of room? (lit. how do you prefer it?)

hay de dos camas there's one with two beds

¿para cuántas noches? for how many nights?

6 *Booking into a campsite*

Pepe ¿Dónde podemos acampar?
Carmen Al final hay mucho sitio libre. ¿Qué traen?
Pepe ¿Cómo?
Carmen ¿Traen ustedes coche y tienda?
Pepe Coche y caravana.
Carmen ¿Cuántas personas son?
Pepe Dos adultos y cuatro niños.
Carmen ¿Qué edad tienen los niños?
Pepe Una tiene más de catorce años y los otros son de . . . menos
de . . . son de trece, doce y diez años.
Carmen Entonces son tres adultos y tres niños.
Pepe Vale.
Carmen ¿Me deja el pasaporte o el carnet de campista?
Pepe Aquí tiene el pasaporte.

al final at the end
(el) sitio place, room
(el) coche car
(la) tienda tent, shop
(la) caravana caravan/trailer
(la) persona person
(el) adulto adult
♦ **catorce** fourteen
♦ **trece** thirteen
♦ **doce** twelve

7 *What's your accommodation like?*

Serafín ¿Está en un hotel o en un apartamento?
Janet Estoy en un apartamento.
Serafín ¿Qué prefiere, un hotel, un apartamento o un camping?
Janet Un apartamento.
Serafín ¿Cómo es el apartamento?
Janet Pues muy bueno. Tiene tres habitaciones, un salón, terraza. Y
usted, ¿está en un hotel?
Serafín Sí, estoy en un gran hotel.
Janet ¿Y cómo es el hotel?
Serafín Pues es un hotel lujoso de cuatro estrellas.
Janet Ah, pues, muy bien.

(el) camping campsite
(el) salón sitting room
(la) terraza terrace

6 ♦ **¿dónde podemos acampar?** where can we camp?

¿qué traen? what have you got with you? (lit. what do you bring with you?)

♦ **¿cómo?** what? Pepe hasn't understood her. If you do not understand what is being said to you, simply say **¿cómo?** it will not be considered impolite.

cuatro niños four children. You've already learnt one word for children **chicos**. **Niños** is another common one and in this context means boys and girls. **Niñas** would refer to a group of girls only.

¿qué edad tienen? how old are they? This is another less common way of saying **¿cuántos años tienen?**

más de catorce años more than fourteen years old. If you're talking about numbers then you must use **más de** if you want to express the idea of more than. The same applies for **menos** = less, **menos de catorce años** less than fourteen years old.

¿me deja el pasaporte? could I have your passport?

el carnet de campista international campers' card. If you're worried about leaving your passport at the campsite office, it's worth having a camper's card for identification.

♦ **aquí tiene el pasaporte** here's my passport. Learn to use the phrase **aquí lo tiene** = here it is, when handing something over (like a passport) to another person; e.g. **su carnet de campista, por favor** = your campers' card, please; **aquí lo tiene**.

7 ♦ **¿cómo es el apartamento?** what's the flat like? **¿Cómo es?** is by far the commonest way of asking what something is like. Janet asks Serafín about the hotel in the same way **¿cómo es el hotel?** what's your hotel like?

estoy en un gran hotel I'm in a big hotel. You've already learnt that **grande** means big; note that when it comes before the word it describes, it is shortened to **gran**; **es una ciudad <u>grande</u>** (it's a big city); **es una <u>gran</u> ciudad**.

es un hotel lujoso de cuatro estrellas it's a luxury four star hotel. The standard of a hotel in Spain is denoted, as in England, by the number of stars it's awarded: the more stars, the more luxurious the hotel.

Key words and phrases

¿qué hay (por aquí)?	what is there (round here)?
¿hay una farmacia por aquí?	is there a chemist's round here?
sí, a la derecha	yes, on the right
sí, a la izquierda	yes, on the left
¿dónde están los servicios?	where are the lavatories?
señoras y caballeros	ladies and gentlemen
al final de la calle	at the end of the street
¿dónde vive/vives?	where do you live?
vivo aquí	I live here
vivo en Madrid	I live in Madrid
¿dónde podemos acampar?	where can we camp?
¿tiene una habitación libre?	have you a room free?
¿qué prefiere/prefieres?	what do you prefer?
sencilla o de matrimonio	single or double (room)
¿para tres noches?	for three nights?
aquí tiene el pasaporte	here's my passport
¿cómo es el hotel?	what's the hotel like?

also note

¿cómo?	what/pardon?
sin	without
bueno	well
para	for

and these numbers

once	eleven
doce	twelve
trece	thirteen
catorce	fourteen
quince	fifteen
dieciséis	sixteen
diecisiete	seventeen
dieciocho	eighteen
diecinueve	nineteen
veinte	twenty

Practice what you have learned

1 First listen to the tape. You will hear a version of the game that Miguel and Pepe were playing earlier. If you can see the objects that Eloisa mentions, in the illustrations below, circle them. Answers on p. 48.

2 On tape you will hear a conversation between a hotel receptionist and a guest. Tick those features that the client's room has. Answers on p. 48.

Una noche

3 Listen to the conversation on tape. The two people in the hotel both have different requirements. Link up each person with what he or she needs, by drawing a line between the person and the facility on offer. Answers on p. 48.

4 On tape you will hear a conversation between two friends about María's holiday apartment. If it has any of the facilities mentioned below, then tick the corresponding box. Answers on p. 48.

terraza
jardín
salón
dos dormitorios
ducha
baño
cama de matrimonio
dos camas

5 The following phrases from a conversation have been jumbled up. First try putting them into a sensible order and then check your answers against those on tape.

¿libre hay sitio? ....

mucho final hay al. ....

¿personas cuántas son? ....

personas tres. ....

bien. deja el me camping carnet de ....

tiene lo aquí ....

Grammar

Vivir to live

As you have already learnt, **vivir** belongs to the third type of Spanish verb – those that end in **-ir**. The present tense is given below:

vivo	I live	**vivimos**	we live
vives	you live (informal)	**vivís**	you live (informal)
vive	he/she lives	**viven**	they live
vive	you live (formal)	**viven**	you live (formal)

1   **Escribir** to write also follows the same pattern. Following the example above, try writing out its present tense. Answers on p. 48.

....

....

Hay

hay	there is	**¿hay?**	is there?
	there are		are there?
no hay	there isn't	**¿no hay?**	isn't there?
	there aren't		aren't there?

hay is simple to use because it doesn't change its form:

hay una botella en la mesa there's a bottle on the table
hay dos botellas en la mesa there are two bottles on the table

If you want to ask a question instead e.g. is there a bank around here? simply change the intonation of your voice to one that implies a question **¿hay un banco por aquí?** When you listen again to the dialogues, note the change in tone when **hay** is used in questions and statements.

Preferir to prefer

This is an irregular verb because it gains an extra **i** before the **e** in some of its parts. There are other verbs which behave in this way – look out for them. It's a good idea to learn the present tense of **preferir** by heart as you will need to use it when making choices in restaurants, hotels etc.

prefiero	I prefer	**preferimos**	we prefer
prefieres	you prefer (informal)	**preferís**	you prefer (informal)
prefiere	he/she prefers	**prefieren**	they prefer
prefiere	you prefer (formal)	**prefieren**	you prefer (formal)

Un, una

El and **la**, **los** and **las** are the masculine and feminine singular and plural forms of 'the'; 'a' also has two forms in the singular:
un señor a man   **una señora** a woman
and two forms in the plural:
unos señores some men   **unas señoras** some women
Note that as in the above example, **unos** and **unas** mean 'some'. If **un** is separated from the word it describes it reverts to its full form **uno** – one.
un amigo a friend   **uno de mis amigos** a friend of mine; one of my friends.

Read and understand

AGENCIA INMOBILARIA
FERNANDEZ

Calle Princesa: vendemos casa, cuatro dormitorios, salón, comedor, terraza, jardín grande, baño, teléfono, cocina Pesetas 5.800.000

Calle Aragón: piso, dos dormitorios, cocina amueblada, baño y ducha, garaje, salón muy grande, cerca club naútico. Pesetas 3.150.000

Calle Forti: Piso pequeño, un dormitorio, baño, cocina, salón, 5 minutos del centro. Pesetas 2.550.000

(la) agencia inmobilaria real estate agents
(el) comedor dining room
(la) cocina amueblada equipped kitchen
(el) teléfono telephone
(un) garaje garage
(el) club naútico sailing club

Now answer the following questions by ticking the appropriate box. Answers on p. 48.

1 The flat on calle Forti is

a. large

b. pretty

c. small

2 How many rooms are there in the flat on calle Aragón?

a. three

b. two

c. five

3 Which of the properties listed in the above advertisement offer separate living and dining rooms?

a. calle Princesa

b. calle Aragón

c. calle Forti

Did you know?

Campsites

Campsites are called **campings** in Spain. Camping is popular now among Spaniards and campsites can become very crowded in the summer, so do book in advance by writing direct to the campsite.

Most campsites are situated along the coast and those inland are few and far between. You can camp off-site with the permission of the authorities or landowners; however, there are a number of regulations governing where you can or cannot camp – the Spanish Tourist Office in New York and Chicago have details, so check with them before travelling abroad.

Campsites are fairly sophisticated in Spain and you can choose between four different categories – even third-class campsites have showers, electricity and gas.

Hotels

There are an enormous number of different types of hotels and guest houses in Spain and a list of the accommodation facilities in the town or district can usually be obtained from the local tourist office. Hotels are divided into five classes (and awarded stars accordingly) and **pensiones** (small family-run establishments) are graded into three categories. A **pensión** might also be referred to as a **fonda**, a **casa de huéspedes** or an **hostal** and they do have the advantage of being both cheap and central.

In addition to these a chain of lodging places has been set up by the Secretariat of State for Tourism in areas of special interest all over Spain. These establishments are of three types: **paradores** which in the main are buildings of artistic or historic value, refurbished to provide all the comforts of a first-class hotel (these are relatively expensive); **albergues de carreterra** are modern hotels located near the main roads which provide the motorist with a comfortable 'stop-over' point; and lastly **refugios** located in beautiful countryside settings.

All prices are fixed centrally so there is little chance of your being tricked into paying too much. The cost of the room is displayed in the room itself (usually on the back of the door): it is for the room itself, per night and not per person, breakfast is usually extra and therefore optional.

Hotels and campsites are required by law to keep and produce complaint forms (**hojas de reclamaciones**) when required to do so by a client. Should you need to make a complaint, fill in one of these forms and you can be sure it will be investigated.

Your turn to speak

You are at a hotel's reception desk and you need a room for the night. Tell the receptionist what you need. You will be practising all the vocabulary necessary for making a booking.

Answers

Practice what you have learned p. 43 Exercise 1 pan; una botella de Coca-Cola; juguetes; lápiz; reloj; un paquete de cigarillos; crema para la piel.

p. 43 Exercise 2 habitación para una noche; ducha; dos camas; terraza.

p. 44 Exercise 3 The man would like: una habitación para una noche, con ducha y dos camas, en el segundo piso. The woman would like: una habitación para tres noches, con ducha, cama de matrimonio, en el primer piso.

p. 44 Exercise 4 Maria's apartment has un salón, una terraza, ducha, dos dormitorios, uno con dos camas, otro con cama de matrimonio.

Grammar p. 45 Exercise 1 escribo, escribes, escribe, escribimos, escribís, escriben.

Read and understand p, 46 1(c); 2(c); 3(a)

4 Ordering drinks and snacks

What you will learn

- understanding what drinks and snacks are available
- understanding questions about what type of drink or snack you prefer
- ordering drinks and snacks
- something about typical drinks and snacks in Spain
- understanding numbers from 20 – 1000

Before you begin

The study guide in this unit is similar to those you have already followed. Try, as far as possible, to work aloud – you are much more likely to be able to say the correct word when you need it, if you have practised saying it aloud beforehand. Remember that you do not have to do the whole unit at one sitting; in fact the best advice for language learners is 'little and often' – ten minutes a day is better than an hour once a week. Before beginning on this unit, if there have been any exercises in the previous three units about which you are still unsure, go back now and do them again.

Study guide

To obtain the maximum benefit from the material in this unit, work through the stages set out below. If you wish, tick them off as you complete each one.

	Dialogues 1 – 3: listen straight through without the book
	Dialogues 1 – 3: listen, read and study one by one
	Dialogues 4 – 6: listen straight through without the book
	Dialogues 4 – 6: listen, read and study one by one
	Study the *Key words and phrases*
	Do the exercises in *Practice what you have learned*
	Study *Grammar*
	Complete *Read and understand*
	Read *Did you know?*
	Do the tape exercise in *Your turn to speak*
	Listen to all the dialogues again without the book

Dialogues

1 *Pepe and Mari Carmen play a counting game*

Pepe	¿Cuánto dinero tienes en la mano?
Mari Carmen	Yo, (eh) cincuenta y cinco
Pepe	Cincuenta y cinco pesetas. Y ahora ¿cuánto dinero tienes?
Mari Carmen	Sesenta.
Pepe	Y este dinero ¿de quién es?
Mari Carmen	Tuyo.

(el) dinero money
cincuenta y cinco fifty-five
sesenta sixty
tuyo yours

2 *Asking for the bill*

Pepe	Oiga, oiga, ¿cuánto es todo?
Camarera	¿Cómo dice señor?
Pepe	La cuenta por favor.
Camarera	Trescientas cuarenta.

camarera waitress
(la) cuenta bill
trescientas cuarenta three hundred and forty

3 *Adding up*

Pepe	¿Cuánto dinero hay en la mesa, Miguel?
Miguel	Hay cinco moneda(s) de cinco peseta(s) que son veinticinco peseta(s). Y luego se le(s) suman cuatro moneda(s) de cinco peseta(s) y hacen un total de cuarenta y cinco peseta(s). Y aquí otra(s) cuanta(s), (sí) otra(s) cinco más, que son cuarenta y cinco peseta(s).

cuarenta y cinco forty-five

1　¿de quién es? whose is it? (lit. of whom is it?) Look out for all the different ways of asking questions in this unit. They will be listed on p. 59.

2　♦　¡oiga! excuse me! (lit. listen!) This is the correct way to attract a waiter's and indeed anyone else's attention.

　♦　¿cómo dice? what did you say? A slightly longer version of the more commonly used ¿cómo? = what?

3　hay cinco monedas de cinco pesetas, que son veinticinco pesetas there are five five-peseta pieces, which make twenty-five pesetas. Note that in reply to the question ¿cuánto es? = how much is it? you should reply son; son trece pesetas it's thirteen pesetas; son dos mil pesetas it's two thousand pesetas.

luego se les suman then you add.

hacen un total that makes a total of . . . hacer = to do/to make.

otras cuantas a few others, some others. Here's another variant of cuanto used in the plural, it means 'some' or 'a few'.

más cinco plus five. Note that Miguel adds up using the word más = more.

4 *Carmen warns Mari Carmen not to drink the water*

Carmen   No, no es potable.
Mari Carmen   Ah no – yo quiero beber.
Carmen   ¡Qué no! que no es agua potable. No se puede beber.

agua potable drinking water
(el) agua water

5 *Pepe has a meal with a Spanish family*

Neni   Alvaro, ¿quieres helado?
Alvaro   ¿De qué son lo(s) helado(s)?
Neni   De naranja y de caramelo. ¿De cuál quieres?
Alvaro   De naranja y de caramelo.
Neni   ¿De los dos?

Neni   ¿Queréis alguno café?
Pedro   Yo.
Pepe   ¿Solo o con leche?
Neni   Como quieras.
Pepe   Para mí con leche.
Neni   ¿Para tí?
Pedro   Solo.
Neni   En seguida lo(s) traigo.

(la) naranja orange
(el) caramelo caramel

4 **yo quiero beber** I want to drink. To ensure that you get what you want you must know and be able to use the verb **querer** = to want/to wish see p. 59.

no se puede beber you can't drink it.

5 ‣ **¿quieres helado?** do you want ice-cream? When asking you for your order, the waiter could phrase things differently. He might for instance ask:
‣ **¿qué quiere de primero?** what would you like as a first course?
‣ **¿qué quiere de segundo?** what would you like as a second course?
‣ **¿qué quiere de postre?** what would you like for dessert?
‣ **¿de qué son los helados?** what sort of ice creams are they? (lit. of what are the ice creams?) Remember that there will be a list of question words in the grammar section on page 59.

¿de cuál quieres? what sort do you want? (lit. of which do you want?) Here's another question word **¿cuál?** = which?

¿queréis alguno café? does anyone want coffee? You must be able to reply to this or similar questions:
‣ **para mí, café con leche** white coffee for me (lit. coffee with milk)
‣ **para mí, café solo** black coffee for me (lit. coffee on its own) Note that you should use **para mí** = for me to express the idea 'I'll have'. If you want to order a black coffee, simply leave out **para mí** and say **café solo**; similarly if you want to order a white coffee say **café con leche**.

como quieras as you like. Don't worry that **quieras** isn't **quieres** as you might expect. Simply note that in certain cases the verb takes a form called the subjunctive.

¿para tí? and for you? In a restaurant, you'll hear
‣ **¿para usted?** Pedro and Neni are husband and wife so they obviously use the less formal **tú**.

en seguida los traigo I'll bring them straightaway. You have already met **traer** in the camping scene in Unit 3. **¿qué traen ustedes?** what have you got with you?/what have you brought with you? **en seguida** = straightaway/immediately.

6 *Ordering drinks and snacks*

Camarero Buenos días, ¿qué desean, señores?

Pepe No sé – ¿qué prefiere usted, don Antonio?

Antonio Yo, vino – ¿y usted?

Pepe No sé, (eh) no sé . . . si prefiero vino o cerveza ahora. ¿Qué hora es, María Luisa?

Luisa Las doce y media.

Pepe Bueno entonces, cerveza.

Camarero Bien, entonces, una cerveza y un vaso de vino ¿tinto o blanco?

Antonio Tinto.

Camarero ¿Y usted señorita?

Luisa Para mí, cerveza también.

Camarero Y de tapas ¿qué desean?

Luisa ¿Qué tienen?

Camarero Bueno, tenemos jamón, queso, ensaladilla, calamares . . .

Pepe ¿Calamares fritos?

Camarero Sí, fritos.

Pepe (Eh) Calamares fritos para mí entonces.

Luisa Sí, para mí, también.

(la) cerveza beer	(el) queso cheese
(el) vaso glass	(la) ensaladilla Russian salad
(la) tapa hors d'oeuvres	(los) calamares squid
(el) jamón ham	frito fried

6 ◗ ¿qué desean? what would you like? If you are on your own in a restaurant you will be asked ¿qué desea?

◗ ¿qué prefiere usted? what would you like? preferir = to prefer.

◗ si prefiero vino o cerveza if I prefer wine or beer.

¿qué hora es? what time is it?

las doce y media half past twelve.

Key words and phrases

¡oiga!	excuse me!
¿qué desea/desean?	
¿qué quiere/quieren?	what would you like?
¿qué prefiere usted?	
¿quiere helado?	would you like an ice cream?
¿qué quiere de primero?	what would you like as a first course?
¿qué quiere de segundo?	what would you like as a second course?
¿qué quiere de postre?	what would you like for dessert?
prefiero un café solo	I prefer a black coffee
yo quiero. . .	I want. . .
beber	to drink
cerveza	beer
¿para usted?	for you?
para mí. . .	for me. . .
café con leche	white coffee
¿de qué es el helado?	what sort of ice cream is it?
¿cuánto es?	how much is it?
¿cómo dice?	what did you say?
la cuenta, por favor	the bill, please
¿de quién es?	whose is it?

and these numbers:

treinta	thirty
cuarenta	forty
cincuenta	fifty
sesenta	sixty
setenta	seventy
ochenta	eighty
noventa	ninety
cien	one hundred
doscientos (-as)	two hundred
trescientos (-as)	three hundred
cuatrocientos (-as)	four hundred
quinientos (-as)	five hundred
seiscientos (-as)	six hundred
setecientos (-as)	seven hundred
ochocientos (-as)	eight hundred
novecientos (-as)	nine hundred
mil	one thousand

Practice what you have learned

1 You will hear a dialogue on your cassette between a waitress and a couple of customers in the Bar Marbella. Reproduced below is the Bar Marbella's menu – tick what the customers order. Numbers from 21 – 1000 are listed on p. 224. Answers on p. 62.

BAR MARBELLA			
zumo de naranja	*40*	*bocadillos*	
cerveza – caña	*40*	*queso*	*160*
– botellín	*50*	*jamón*	*185*
vino (vaso)	*30*	*sardinas*	*170*
whisky	*80*	*tapas variadas*	
café con leche	*40*	*calamares*	*150*
café solo	*35*	*ensaladilla*	*126*
pan	*20*	*helados*	*90*
agua mineral	*30*		

(el) zumo juice
(la) caña draught (beer)
(el) botellín bottle
(el) bocadillo sandwich
(la) sardina sardine

2 Now for the bill. Some of the words are omitted in the transcript below. Listen carefully to the tape and then fill in the blanks. (Answers on p. 62.)

Cliente ¡ .... camarero!

Camarero Sí ....

Cliente La .... por favor.

Camarero ¿Cómo ....?

Cliente ¿ .... es?

Camarero .... cuatrocientas cuarenta pesetas.

Cliente Bien, tenga.

Camarero .... señora.

3 Listen to the tape. You will be given change in three different shops by the assistant. How much did you get in each shop? Tick the correct box. You'll probably have to listen to the tape two or three times in order to work out the answers. Answers on p. 62.

1 **a.** veinticinco pesetas ☐

   b. cuatrocientas pesetas ☐

   c. doscientas cuarenta pesetas ☐

2 **a.** cuarenta y cinco pesetas ☐

   b. cincuenta pesetas ☐

   c. treinta y cinco pesetas ☐

3 **a.** ciento sesenta y cinco pesetas ☐

   b. ciento cincuenta y cinco pesetas ☐

   c. ciento sesenta pesetas ☐

4 On your tape you will hear a waiter adding up bills for three separate tables. It takes him a little time to add up. Try adding up the sums yourself: press the pause button after he says **son** e.g. **dos y dos son** (pause) **cuatro** then start the cassette again to hear if you were right. Write in the final sum for each table in the box below and then check your answers against those on p. 62.

BAR MARBELLA	
Mesa	*Precio*
1	
2	
3	

(el) precio price

5 In the dialogue below between a waiter and a customer, the customer's part hasn't been printed. Can you complete the conversation, choosing the correct response from the box below? (Answers on p. 62.)

Camarero Buenos días, señora ¿qué desea?

Señora ¿ .... ?

Camarero Sí, claro.

Señora ¿ .... ?

Camarero Son de naranja, de caramelo y de café.

Señora ....

Camarero ¿Algo más?

Señora ......¿ .... ?

Camarero Pues tenemos bocadillos de queso y de jamón

Señora ....

Camarero Bien, y ¿café, zumos?

Señora ....

Camarero ¿Solo o con leche?

Señora ....

¿De qué son?

Pues un helado de café

Sí, ¿qué bocadillos tiene?

Un café por favor

Un bocadillo de jamón entonces.

Solo, por favor

¿Hay helados?

Grammar

Asking questions

a. You can simply change the tone of your voice so that a statement becomes a question.

hay pan there is bread   **¿hay pan?** is there any bread?

b. You can add **¿verdad?** or **¿no?** = isn't that so?/right? to the end of your sentence.

aquí ¿no? here, isn't that right?

y nada más ¿verdad? and nothing else, right?

c. You can change the order of the verb and the pronoun so that

usted tiene una habitación you've got a room becomes

¿tiene usted una habitación? do you have a room?

d. You can use a question word at the beginning of a sentence like *how? where? what sort? how much?* Listed below are some of the ones which appeared in this unit. Can you remember what all these questions mean?

¿cuánto dinero tienes?   ¿de quién es?   ¿cómo dice?   ¿qué quiere?   ¿de cuál quiere?   ¿de qué son?

If not, look back at the *Key words and phrases.*

Note: **porque** can mean both why? and because. How do you tell the difference? Either from the tone of voice or in written Spanish simply from the spelling **porque** = because and **¿por qué?** = why?

Querer to want

This verb does not follow the usual **-er** pattern.

quiero	queremos
quieres	queréis
quiere	quieren

Numbers

21 – 29 in numerical order they are: **veintiuno, veintidós, veintitrés, veinticuatro, veinticinco, veintiséis, veintisiete, veintiocho, veintinueve.**

31 – 39: again in numerical order: **treinta y uno, treinta y dos, treinta y tres, treinta y cuatro, treinta y cinco, treinta y seis, treinta y siete, treinta y ocho, treinta y nueve.** This is the pattern followed by all other numbers up to 100.

Note: *1 – 100*: the only numbers that change their endings are those that end in **-uno**: they must agree with the gender of the word they accompany – *never* make them plural:

veintiuna pesetas twenty-one pesetas   **veintiún señores** twenty-one men

100: if there are exactly one hundred things use **cien**: **cien pesetas** one hundred pesetas

if there are more use **ciento**: **ciento una pesetas** one hundred and one pesetas

NB: if talking about one hundred *and* three, use **ciento tres** not **ciento y tres.**

200 – 900: these numbers must agree with the word that follows them

doscientas pesetas 200 pesetas   **trescientos hombres** 300 men

doscientas ochenta y ocho pesetas 288 pesetas

Read and understand

The menu below is taken from the Cafetería Bristol. Read it through carefully.

CAFETERIA BRISTOL

1° GRUPO		2° GRUPO	
sopa de tomate	80	tortilla de queso	180
ensaladilla	175	tortilla de jamón	200
sardinas con tomate	150	trucha con jamón	250
entremeses variados	100	gambas a la plancha	275
huevos fritos	125		
calamares	160		

3° GRUPO

Flan	75
Helados variados	85

VARIOS

pan	20
agua mineral	55
café	40
cerveza	90

(la) **sopa de tomate** tomato soup
(los) **entremeses variados** hors d'oeuvres
(los) **huevos fritos** fried eggs
(la) **tortilla** Spanish omelet
(la) **trucha** trout
(las) **gambas a la plancha** grilled prawns
(el) **flan** cream caramel

Look at the chit from the Cafetería Bristol. The waiter has only entered the prices. Can you fill in the order? Answers on p. 62.

CAFETERIA BRISTOL

....	80
....	125
....	200
....	250
....	75
....	85
....	55
....	90

UNIT 4

Did you know?

Bars and cafés

You may remember that in this unit Pepe attracted the waiter's attention by calling ¡**Oiga**! This may sound abrupt but it is perfectly acceptable. Previously the customer could also clap his hands or hiss but this is now frowned upon.

Tapas are offered with pre-lunch or pre-dinner drinks. These used to be free but you may well find yourself being charged for them in the tourist spots. They are a good way of sampling regional dishes without committing yourself to a meal – typical offerings include **tortilla** (Spanish omelet), **aceitunas** (olives), **calamares** (squid) and **boquerones** (rather like unsalted anchovies). **Raciones** are rather larger portions which you must order yourself and pay for.

If you keep reordering drinks, keep your chits as the waiter will total them up at the end of the evening. Tipping is still common practice in Spain even though service might already have been included on the bill. In a bar between 2 – 5 pesetas is quite enough for the barman; sometimes the bar counter has a jug or box marked **bote** where you should place your tip. The money is then divided up at the end of the evening between all the waiters. By the way, you will be charged slightly more if you sit at a table rather than stand at the bar.

Restaurants

Like hotels, restaurants are also categorized. They are awarded between one and five forks (**tenedores**). Meals are served much later than in the U.S. Few Spaniards would consider sitting down to lunch before 2 p.m. and many eat at 3 p.m. Some hotels catering to foreign visitors have adapted their meal times to suit clients. Lunch (**la comida** or **el almuerzo**) is considered to be the main meal of the day and will consist of three courses, wine, coffee and liqueurs. Dinner (**la cena**) will be served at around 9.30 p.m. – 10 p.m. and is a much lighter meal. Many restaurants do not open before 9.30 p.m. so do check on times before setting out to look for somewhere to eat.

By law, menus must be displayed outside or in the window of the restaurant and that is the only way to judge if a place is right for your needs. Self-service restaurants (**autoservicios**) are not unknown but all other establishments have waiter service. As in the U.S., it is usual to leave 10% to 15% of the bill for the waiter.

If you can't wait until 9:30 p.m. for your evening meal try a **casa de comidas** or a **mesón** which will provide a meal in the early evenings – **merienda** – rather like a snack without sweet things!

And finally, be prepared to wait!

Your turn to speak

It's now your turn to go into a Spanish restaurant and order lunch.

You are in a restaurant, taking the parts of both customers. Isabel will not be prompting you. Instead use the illustrations below as your 'prompts' in the numerical order shown.

Answers

Practice what you have learned p. 56 Exercise **1**
botellín; zumo de naranja; un bocadillo de queso; calamares fritos

p. 56 Exercise **2** ¡Oiga, camarero! Sí, señora. La cuenta, por favor.
¿Cómo dice? ¿Cuánto es? Son cuatrocientas cuarenta pesetas. Bien, tenga.
Gracias, señora.
p. 57 Exercise **3** (**1**) c; (**2**) b; (**3**) a.

p. 57 Exercise **4** table 1 = 165 pesetas; table 2 = 260 pesetas; table 3 = 140 pesetas.

p. 58 Exercise **5** Buenos días, señora ¿qué desea?/¿Hay helados?/Sí, claro./¿De qué son?/Son de naranja, de caramelo y de café./Pues un helado de café./¿Algo más?/Sí, ¿qué bocadillos tiene?/Pues tenemos bocadillos de queso y de jamón./Un bocadillo de jamón entonces./Bien, y ¿café, zumos . . .?/Un café por favor./¿Solo o con leche?/Solo, por favor.

Read and understand p. 60 sopa de tomate; huevos fritos; tortilla de jamón; trucha con jamón; flan; helados; agua mineral; cerveza.

5 Directions

What you will learn

- asking for directions
- understanding the instructions you are given
- asking about distances
- asking what road signs mean
- something about driving in Spain

Before you begin

Asking the way is relatively easy: it is understanding the answer that tends to prove more of a problem! The best way round this is to listen over and over again to the directions given in the dialogue, so that you will understand the *key* phrases (*straight ahead, the first turn* etc.) even if they are obscured by other words that you do not know. It is usually a good idea to repeat directions as soon as you are given them, so that you can be corrected if you have misunderstood anything.

There will be an opportunity for revision at the end of this unit, but you should also get into the habit of looking back over what you have learnt – and redoing exercises that you are not sure of.

Study guide

	Dialogues 1 – 4: listen straight through, without the book
	Dialogues 1 – 4: listen, read, and study one by one
	Dialogues 5 – 7: listen straight through without the book
	Dialogues 5 – 7: listen, read and study one by one
	Study the *Key words and phrases*
	Do the exercises in *Practice what you have learned*
	Study the *Grammar* section and do the exercise
	Complete *Read and understand*
	Read *Did you know?*
	Do the tape exercise in *Your turn to speak*
	Finally, listen to all the dialogues again straight through
	Do the revision/review exercises on p. 217

Dialogues

1 *What does this sign mean?*

Pepe ¿Qué significa esta señal?
Neni No se puede circular por esta calle.
Pepe ¿Y qué significa esta señal?
Neni No se puede circular en bicicleta por esta calle.
Pepe ¿Y qué significa esta señal?
Neni No se puede aparcar.
Pepe ¿Y qué significa esta señal?
Neni No se puede circular a más de cuarenta.
Pepe ¿Qué significa esta señal?
Pedro No se puede girar a la derecha.
Pepe ¿Y ésta?
Pedro No se puede girar a la izquierda.

(la) bicicleta bicycle
aparcar to park

2 *How far is it to . . . ?*

Pepe ¿A cuántos kilómetros está Jerez?
Ricardo A unos ochenta y cinco kilómetro(s).
Pepe ¿Y a cuántos kilómetros está Córdoba?
Ricardo Mucho más lejo(s). A dosciento(s) kilómetro(s).

lejos far

3 *How to get to the Plaza Mayor*

Pepe ¿Cómo se puede ir a la Plaza Mayor?
Gallega En autobús o en metro.
Pepe ¿No se puede ir a pie?
Gallega Sí, pero está muy lejos.
Pepe ¿Se puede ir en autobús desde aquí?
Gallega Sí.

(el) autobús bus
(el) metro tube, underground, subway
ir a pie to walk (lit. to go on foot)

1 ♦ **¿qué significa esta señal?** what does this sign mean?

no se puede circular por esta calle traffic prohibited in this street (lit. one cannot travel down this street).

no se puede girar a la derecha no right turn (lit. one cannot turn right).

no se puede girar a la izquierda no left turn. **girar** is one word for to turn, **doblar** is another and one which you will probably hear more frequently: **doblar la esquina** to turn the corner; **doble a la derecha** turn right.

2 ♦ **¿a cuántos kilómetros está Jerez?** how far is Jerez? (lit. at how many kilometres distance is Jerez?)

a unos ochenta y cinco kilómetros about eighty-five kilometres away. Note how, as in English, **unos** some/about is used here to give an idea of approximation. **Hay unas cincuenta personas aquí** there are about fifty people here.

3 ♦ **¿cómo se puede ir?** how do you get to? The verb that follows **se puede** is always in the infinitive **¿se puede comer aquí?** can one eat here? As you have seen in dialogue 1, verbs which follow **no se puede** must also be in the infinitive: **no se puede comer aquí** you cannot eat here.

♦ **¿se puede ir en autobús desde aquí?** can you go by bus from here? **desde** is an alternative to **de** = from. Its opposite is **hasta** until, which also has the alternative **a** = to: **desde hoy hasta el fin de semana** from today until the weekend; **de miércoles a viernes** from Wednesday to Friday.

4 *Which way to the Plaza de la Magdalena?*

Pepe   Por favor, ¿la Plaza de la Magdalena?
Ernesto La segunda bocacalle a la derecha.

5 *And to the Plaza Mayor?*

Pepe   Por favor, ¿para ir a la Plaza Mayor?
Recepcionista Toda la calle adelante, Calle Mayor a la izquierda.
Pepe   ¿Está lejos?
Recepcionista Muy cerca.

6 *Which way to Sierpes Street?*

Mari Por favor, ¿me dice cómo se va a la calle Sierpe(s)?
Paco A la calle Sierpe(s), pues . . . tiene que coger la primera calle a la izquierda, después seguir todo recto y al final, te encontrarás con ella.
Mari Gracias
Paco De nada.

Plaza Mayor, Madrid

4 ◆ **la segunda bocacalle a la derecha** the second turn on the right. **Bocacalle** is made up of (**la**) **boca** mouth and **calle** road/street hence literally, **bocacalle** mouth (opening) in the street.

5 ◆ **¿para ir a la Plaza Mayor?** to get to the Main Square? An easy way is to simply name the place that you want to go to **¿la Plaza Mayor, por favor?** **toda la calle adelante** straight on down the street.

6 **¿me dice usted cómo se va a la calle Sierpes?** can you tell me how to get to Sierpes Street? La calle Sierpes is a well-known shopping street in the centre of Seville.

después seguir todo recto y, al final, te encontrarás con ella then you go straight on and at the end you'll find it. **Encontrarse con** to come across: **se encontrará con el bolso** she'll find the handbag. Note how although Mari and Paco begin by addressing each other in the **usted** form, by the end of the dialogue, Paco is addressing Mari in the **tú** form: **te encontrarás**. Grammatical slips of this sort are quite common in the spoken language and, as you can see, do not hinder understanding.

7 *At a service station*

Pepe Oiga, por favor, ¿para ir hacia la carretera de Madrid? ¿Para ir a Madrid?

Gasolinero Bueno, pues tiene usted que salir por la carretera de la nacional uno y está tomando el puente, el puente romano, el puente viejo y después a mano izquierda allí verá los indicadores para Madrid.

Pepe Tengo que cruzar el puente, ¿no?

Gasolinero Sí, sí, tiene que ir al otro lado del río.

Pepe ¿Y luego doblo?

Gasolinero A la izquierda. (A la izquierda) Y allí verá los indicadores para Avila y Madrid.

Pepe Aha. ¿Y tengo que pasar por Avila?

Gasolinero Pues sí, puede usted pasar por Avila, pero no es necesario.

> **(el) gasolinero** gasoline station attendant
> **hacia** towards
> **romano** Roman
> **viejo** old
> **después** then
> **a mano izquierda** on the left hand (**la mano** hand)
> **necesario** necessary

7

tiene usted que salir por la carretera de la nacional uno you have to go out along the N.1 road; **(la) carretera** road.

está tomando el puente you take the bridge. **Tomar** and **coger** to take **tome/coja la carretera a la izquierda** take the road on the left.

allí verá los indicadores there you will see the signs.

♦ **¿tengo que cruzar el puente?** I've got to cross the bridge? Pepe is making sure he has understood the directions he has been given. You'll soon notice when you are given instructions that people use **tiene que** you have to.

al otro lado del río to the other side of the river.

♦ **¿tengo que pasar por Avila?** do I have to go through Avila? There's more about **por** in the grammar section.

Key words and phrases

¿la plaza de la Magdalena, por favor?	Magdalena Square, please?
¿para ir a la plaza de la Magdalena?	how do you get to Magdalena Square?
¿cómo se puede ir a la plaza de la Magdalena?	how does one get to Magdalena Square?
a la derecha	to the right
a la izquierda	to the left
no se puede ir . . .	you can't go. . .
a la derecha	to the right
usted coge la primera bocacalle	you take the first turn
usted coge la segunda bocacalle	you take the second turn
usted coge la tercera bocacalle	you take the third turn
tiene que tomar/coger esta carretera	you've got to take this road
tiene que doblar la esquina	you've got to turn the corner
todo recto/todo seguido	straight ahead
al otro lado de la calle	on the other side of the road
¿está lejos?	is it far?
¿a cuántos kilómetros está?	how many kilometres away is it?
¿tengo que (cruzar el puente)?	do I have to (cross the bridge)?
¿tengo que (pasar por . . .)?	do I have to (go through . . .)?
¿qué significa esta señal?	what does this sign mean?

Practice what you have learned

1 Here is a map of Palencia. On tape you will hear a number of statements about the locations of certain buildings in the town. State whether they are true **verdad** or false **mentira** by ticking the appropriate box. Answers on p. 76.

A Catedral
B Iglesia de San Miguel = Church of St Michael
C Capilla de San Bernardo = Chapel of St Bernard

D Oficina de Información Turismo = Tourist Office
E Telégrafos = Telegraph Office
F Teléfonos = Telephone Exchange

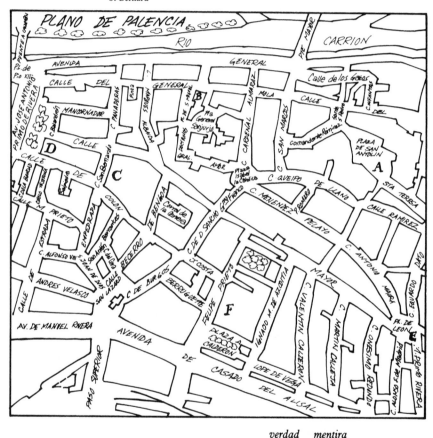

		verdad	mentira
1	Catedral	☐	☐
2	Iglesia de San Miguel	☐	☐
3	Capilla de San Bernardo	☐	☐
4	Oficina de Información Turismo	☐	☐
5	Telégrafos	☐	☐
6	Teléfonos	☐	☐

2 Listen to your tape where you will hear several people being given directions. The diagrams below illustrate what each person must do. Write in the name of the person underneath the appropriate illustration. The names are: Elisa, Juana, Juan and Pablo. Answers on p. 76.

a. .... b. ....

c. .... d. ....

3 Look at the map of Palencia again. Listen carefully to the tape where the locations of various monuments will be given (without the actual monuments being named!) See if you can write down in English where the monuments are and have a guess as to which monument is referred to. Answers on p. 76.

1 ....
....

2 ....
....

3 ....
....

4 ....
....

5 ....
....

4 Below is a map of the roads leading out of Seville. On tape you will be given the distances of various towns from Seville. For example: **Carmona está a unos treinta y tres kilómetros.** Listen to the distances given and then state whether they were correct or incorrect by ticking the appropriate box. Answers on p. 76.

		verdad	*mentira*
1	Osuna	☐	☐
2	Ecija	☐	☐
3	Marchena	☐	☐
4	Utrera	☐	☐
5	Lebrija	☐	☐
6	Morón de la Frontera	☐	☐
7	San Isidoro	☐	☐

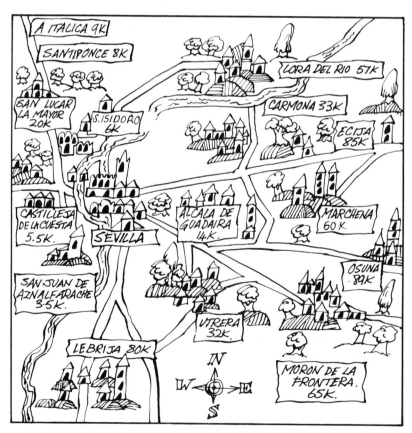

Grammar

Se puede

If you want to say that you can do something – that it's allowed, or is possible – then you use the phrase **se puede** one can. It's always followed by a verb in the infinitive so it's easy to use. It has occurred throughout this unit in phrases like:

¿se puede ir en autobus? can you go by bus?

And of course you simply place **no** in front of **se puede** if you want to say you cannot do something:

no se puede andar aquí you cannot walk here

Por/para

These two words are often translated as 'for' but they are used in different ways and in different situations.
para can mean *in order to*

¿para ir a Marchena? how do I get to Marchena?
¿para ir a la catedral? how does one get to the cathedral?

para can mean *towards*

los indicadores para Avila the signs for Avila

por can mean *through* or *along*

¿tengo que pasar por Avila? do I have to go through Avila?
no se puede circular por esta calle no traffic along this street

It's also used in some set phrases

por favor please   **por aquí** around here

1 Should you use **por** or **para** in the following sentences? Answers on p. 76.

New vocabulary (**la**) **autopista** motorway

a. .... favor, ¿................. ir a la Plaza Mayor?

b. ¿Hay una parada de taxis .... aquí?

c. Allí hay los indicadores .... Segovia.

d. ¿Tengo que pasar .... Palencia?

e. Se puede ir .... la autopista.

Read and understand

Read the following passage out loud once to practise your spoken Spanish and then read it through to yourself until you understand all the directions.

La Plaza del Mercado está cerca del centro de Sevilla. Para ir allí desde la Calle de la Magdalena, se puede ir a pie pero está lejos. Usted tiene que coger la primera calle a la izquierda, que es la Calle Preciados. Al final está la Plaza San Antonio. Luego, todo recto hasta los semáforos. Allí, tiene que doblar a la derecha, y al final de esta calle, está la Plaza del Mercado.

(los) semáforos traffic lights

Under each word in the box below, can you write its opposite? Answers on p. 76.

cerca
....
al principio
....
desde
....
a la derecha
....
en malas condiciones
....

Did you know?

Driving in Spain

Getting around by car is one of the best ways of seeing the country: communications can be poor and the distances between towns can be great! However, there are certain things to remember before you set off: you will need an international driving licence, the car's registration and a U.S. sticker to put on the back of the car. You will also need a 'green card' and a bail bond (which guarantees $800 to the Spanish government in case you have an accident).

If you are involved in an accident and do not have a bail bond both you and your car can be detained by the authorities – no matter how trivial the accident! Your insurance company should supply you with both a 'green card' and a bail bond. You should also carry a portable red triangle as a warning signal in case you have to park the car in an emergency.

There is now a network of motorways in Spain (labelled with the prefix A) and you have to pay a toll – about a peseta per kilometre. Unfortunately, there are no concessions on these tolls for visitors to Spain. Current details on motorway prices can be requested from ASETA, Estebañez Calderón 3, Madrid 20. The network is continually being extended, so do make sure you have an up-to-date map!

There are six main highways leading out of Madrid (labelled N) and numbered with Roman numerals, NIV. Other main roads are also labelled N, but with ordinary numerals, N246. Local roads are labelled C, C654.

The speed limits are as follows: motorways 120 km per hr, national highways 100 km per hr, other roads 90 km per hr *unless otherwise specified* and towns and built-up areas 60 km per hr.

Gasoline

In Spain, gasoline comes in three grades: **extra**, **super**, and **normal**. Although it is 'officially' sold by the litre, you can ask for it in pesetas '**mil pesetas de super**': 'a 1000 pesetas worth of super'. A minimum sale of five litres is often imposed. If you are off the beaten track, it is worth filling up with gasoline where you can because you may not find a gasoline station open when you need it and some service stations do not stock **extra**.

You will be offered more services than is the case in the U.S. – attendants will check your oil and clean your windshield without your having to ask. By the way, gasoline prices are standardized throughout Spain because the sale of gasoline is a state monopoly.

Your turn to speak

You will be asking for directions to the Plaza Mayor.
You will be practising: ¿**se puede ir . . .? tengo que . . .** and
understanding directions.

Revision/Review

Now a chance to go over some of the important language you have learnt in
Units 1 – 5. Turn to the back of the book p. 217 for what to do. You will
also need your tape recorder.

Answers

Practice what you have learned p. 70 Exercise **1** They are all **verdad!**

p. 71 Exercise **2** (**a**) Juana (**b**) Elisa (**c**) Pablo (**d**) Juan

p. 71 Exercise **3** (**1**) Telegraph Office: near the Plaza de Leon (**2**) Tourist
Office: it's in the Avenida José Antonio, Primo de Rivera (**3**) Chapel of
Saint Bernard: it's in the Calle San Bernardo (**4**) Telephone Exchange: it's
very near the Plaza de Calderón (**5**) Church of St Michael: it's close to the
river

p. 72 Exercise **4** (**1**) mentira (**2**) verdad (**3**) mentira (**4**) mentira
(**5**) verdad (**6**) mentira (**7**) mentira

Grammar p. 73 Exercise **1** (**a**) por . . . para (**b**) por (**c**) para (**d**) por
(**e**) por

Read and understand p. 74 cerca/lejos; al principio/al final; desde/hasta; a
la derecha/a la izquierda; en malas condiciones/en buenas condiciones.

6 Time

What you will learn

- telling the time
- the days of the week
- the months of the year
- other useful expressions of time
- coping with timetables
- asking how long a journey takes
- making a telephone call in Spain

Before you begin

Being able to ask and understand *when* things are happening/open/available is essential to the smooth running of a holiday or business trip. Asking the questions is fairly simple; ¿cuándo? when? and ¿a qué hora? at what time? will cover most eventualities. Learn dates, days and times carefully, and practise saying them aloud. For instance, whenever you look at your watch you could try saying the time to yourself in Spanish.

Before you listen to the dialogues, revise the following numbers. Say them out loud in Spanish and then check on them on p. 90: *10, 14, 24, 22, 15, 9, 5, 28, 31, 17, 19, 21*

Study guide

	Dialogues 1 – 5: listen straight through without the book
	Dialogues 1 – 5: listen, read and study one by one
	Dialogues 6 – 9: listen straight through without the book
	Dialogues 6 – 9: listen, read and study one by one
	Study the *Key words and phrases*
	Do the exercises in *Practice what you have learned*
	Study *Grammar*
	Complete *Read and understand*
	Read *Did you know?*
	Do the tape exercise in *Your turn to speak*
	Finally, listen to all the dialogues again straight through

Dialogues

1 *What time is it?*

Pepe ¿Qué hora es por favor?
Javier Son las once menos cinco minutos.
Pepe Gracias.

2 *When do you open/close?*

Pepe Por favor, ¿a qué hora se abre El Corte Inglés?
Loli A las diez de la mañana.
Pepe ¿Y a qué hora se cierra?
Loli A las ocho.
Pepe ¿Todos los días de la semana?
Loli Todos los días de la semana.
Pepe ¿Los sábados también?
Loli Los sábados también.
Pepe ¿Y no cierran ustedes al mediodía?
Loli No, nunca.
Pepe Nunca. ¿Pero los domingos no abren, no?
Loli No, no, nunca.
Pepe Nunca.

(la) semana week   **al mediodía** at midday
nunca never

3 *At what time does the train arrive?*

Pepe Por favor, ¿a qué hora llega el tren de La Coruña?
Dorita A las veintiuna horas catorce minutos.

PROXIMAS LLEGADAS

TREN	PROCEDENCIA	HORA PREVISTA	
EXPRESO	MADRID	08	20
TRANVIA	VALLADOLID	13	55
TRANVIA	MEDINA DEL CAMPO	20	4 4
MADRID	ELECTRO TREN	21	20

1 ◆ **¿qué hora es?** what time is it? Time expressions are dealt with more fully in the grammar section.

◆ **son las once menos cinco minutos** it's five to eleven. Note another use of the word **menos** – here minus (lit. it's eleven o'clock minus five minutes.)

2 ◆ **¿a qué hora se abre El Corte Inglés?** at what time does the Corte Inglés open? This is the most usual way of asking what time shops, offices and bars open. You will be practising it later in the unit.

◆ **¿y a qué hora se cierra?** and at what time does it close?

CERRADO POR VACACIONES Hasta el 22 de Octubre

3 ◆ **¿a qué hora llega el tren de La Coruña?** at what time does the La Coruña train arrive?

◆ **a las veintiuna horas catorce minutos** at 21:14. Although the twenty-four hour clock is not used frequently in conversation, it is used for all timetables, so it is explained fully on page 87.

4 *At what time does the train leave?*

Pepe ¿A qué hora sale el tren para Salamanca, por favor?
Dorita ¿Por la mañana o por la tarde?
Pepe Por la mañana y por la tarde, por favor.
Dorita Tiene uno a las ocho horas quince minutos, semi-directo con llegada a Salamanca a las doce horas treinta minutos, y por la tarde tiene otro semi-directo, a las dieciséis horas quince minutos, con llegada a Salamanca a las veinte horas treinta minutos.
Pepe ¿Por favor, a qué hora llega a Salamanca el de la tarde?
Dorita A las veinte horas treinta minutos.
Pepe ¿Y sale el tren siempre a su hora?
Dorita Sí, sale en punto.
Pepe Gracias.

5 *How long does the journey take?*

Pepe ¿Cuánto dura el viaje a Vigo, por favor?
Dorita Diez horas aproximadamente.
Pepe ¿Cómo?
Dorita Diez horas.
Pepe Y a La Coruña, ¿cuánto tiempo tarda en llegar?
Dorita Diez horas y media.
Pepe Diez horas y media. Gracias.

aproximadamente approximately

6 *When does the bus arrive?*

Pepe ¿A qué hora viene el autobús de Toledo?
Luisa El autobús hoy viene con media hora de retraso.
Pepe ¿Hay autobuses para Cáceres?
Luisa Sí, hay autobuses por la tarde, los lunes, miércoles y viernes.
Pepe ¿Y por la mañana?
Luisa Sí, por la mañana, los martes, los jueves y los sábados.
Pepe ¿Y los domingos?
Luisa No, los domingos no hay autobuses.

los martes Tuesdays
los jueves Thursdays

4 ♦ **¿a qué hora sale el tren para Salamanca, por favor?** at what time does the Salamanca train leave, please? You'll need to know when trains and buses leave, as well as when they arrive!

♦ **¿por la mañana o por la tarde?** in the morning or in the afternoon? However, note that in 'it's eleven o'clock *in the* morning' should be translated as **son las once de la mañana**.

tiene uno a las ocho horas quince minutos there's one at 8:15 (lit. you've got one at 8:15).

semi-directo con llegada a Salamanca it's a semi-direct, with an arrival time at Salamanca of . . . Dorita means that it isn't a through train.

¿el de la tarde? the afternoon train? (lit. the one of the afternoon) Pepe hasn't bothered repeating the word **tren** train.

¿sale el tren siempre a su hora? does the train always leave on time? Pepe has obviously had a lot of experience with trains! Dorita uses another expression for 'on time' **sale en punto** it leaves on the dot.

5 **¿cuánto dura el viaje a Vigo?** how long does the journey to Vigo take? However, the more common expression and the one you should concentrate on is

♦ **¿cuánto tiempo tarda en llegar?** (lit. how long does it take to arrive?) You will be practising this expression later in the unit.

6 ♦ **¿a qué hora viene el autobús de Toledo?** at what time does the Toledo bus arrive?

viene con media hora de retraso it's half an hour late (lit. it's coming with half an hour's delay) **(el) retraso** delay.

♦ **los lunes, miércoles y viernes** Mondays, Wednesdays and Fridays. This dialogue cunningly names all the days of the week!

7 *Making a telephone call*

Pepe Por favor, quiero hacer una llamada a Wolverhampton. ¿Qué tengo que hacer, por favor?
Telefonista ¿Para dónde?
Pepe Wolverhampton, en Inglaterra.
Telefonista En Inglaterra. ¿Sabe usted el número de la ciudad?
Pepe El nueve cero dos.
Telefonista Pue(s) entonce(s) tiene que marcar el cero siete, esperar el tono, el cuatro, cuatro, nueve, cero, do(s) y el del abonado.

8 *A guessing game*

Pepe ¿Quién es éste?
Neni El presidente del gobierno español.
Pepe ¿Y quién es ésta?
Neni La reina de España, doña Sofía.
Pepe ¿Y quién es éste?
Neni Su esposo, el rey don Juan Carlos de España.

9 *Saints' days and birthdays*

Pepe Oye, ¿cuándo es tu cumpleaños?
María Luisa Mi cumpleaños es el veintiocho de agosto.
Pepe El veintiocho de agosto, y ¿cómo te llamas?
María Luisa María Luisa.
Pepe ¿Y cuándo es el día de tu santo? ¿No es lo mismo, no?
María Luisa No, no, el día de mi santo es el veintiuno de julio, San Luís.

7 ♦ **quiero hacer una llamada a Wolverhampton** I want to make a call to Wolverhampton.

tiene que marcar el cero siete, esperar el tono you should dial zero seven, wait for the dialling tone.

el del abonado the telephone number of the subscriber.

8 **¿quién es éste?** who is this?

el presidente del gobierno español the president of the Spanish government.

¿quién es ésta? who is this? See p. 87 for further details on pronouns but note here how the endings of **éste/ésta** change according to whether 'this' refers to something masculine or feminine. Note also **aquel** 'that' **¿quién es aquél?** who is that? The ending of **aquel** also changes according to whether the subject is female **¿quién es aquella chica?** who is that girl?

la reina de España, doña Sofía the Queen of Spain, doña Sofía.

su esposo, el rey don Juan Carlos de España her husband, King Juan Carlos of Spain.

9 ♦ **oye, ¿cuándo es tu cumpleaños?** hey (lit. listen) when's your birthday? **¿Cuándo es?** is another useful question word – remember the list in Unit 5. (**el**) **cumpleaños** may look plural, but it is a singular.

el día de tu santo your saint's day. Most Spaniards are christened with the name of a saint and they tend to celebrate these days more than their birthdays.

¿no es lo mismo, no? it's not the same, is it? Note this use of **no ¿no es el presidente, no?** it's not the president, is it?

Key words and phrases

¿qué hora es?
what time is it?

son (las diez de la noche)
it's (ten o'clock at night)

¿a qué hora se abre (El Corte Inglés)?
at what time time does (El Corte Inglés) open?

a las ocho de la mañana
at eight o'clock in the morning

a las cuatro de la tarde
at four o'clock in the afternoon

¿a qué hora se cierra (el bar) (por la noche)?
at what time does (the bar) close (at night)?

a las once de la noche
at eleven o'clock at night

¿a qué hora viene el autobús?
at what time does the bus arrive?

¿a qué hora sale el autobús para Valencia?
at what time does the bus leave for Valencia?

¿cuánto tiempo tarda en llegar?
how long does it take to arrive?

dos horas
two hours

¿cuándo es (su cumpleaños)?
when is (your birthday)?

el veintidós de setiembre
the twenty-second of September

quiero (hacer una llamada a . . .)
I want (to make a call to . . .)

¿por la mañana o por la tarde?
in the morning or in the afternoon?

Days of the week:

lunes — Monday
martes — Tuesday
miércoles — Wednesday
jueves — Thursday
viernes — Friday
sábado — Saturday
domingo — Sunday

Months of the year:

enero — January
febrero — February
marzo — March
abril — April
mayo — May
junio — June

julio — July
agosto — August
setiembre — September
octubre — October
noviembre — November
diciembre — December

Times:

¿qué hora es? — what time is it?
es la una — it's one o'clock
son las dos — it's two o'clock
son las tres y cinco — it's five past three
son las cuatro y diez — it's ten past four
son las cinco y cuarto — it's quarter past five
son las seis y media — it's half past six
son las siete menos veinticinco — it's twenty-five to seven
son las ocho menos cuarto — it's a quarter to eight
son las nueve menos diez — it's ten to nine

¿a qué hora (se abre)? — at what time (does it open)?
a las dos — at two o'clock
a las tres y cinco — at five past three

Practice what you have learned

1 On tape you will hear Miguel Gómez asking the girl at the ticket office (**la taquillera**) about times of trains from Palma to Soller. Fill in the details (writing out the times in full) in the timetable below. You will certainly have to use your pause button for this exercise. Answers on p. 90.

> ## TRENES
>
> Salidas de Palma para Soller
>
> **a.** ....
>
> **b.** ....
>
> **c.** ....
>
> **d.** ....
>
> **e.** ....

2 On tape you will hear two short dialogues. The sentences below are in the wrong order – as are the words within the sentences! Can you put them into the correct order? Check your answers by listening to the tape again.

a. media y las a ocho   ....

     ¿dónde el de tren?   ....

     Salamanca de   ....

     ¿tren llega qué a hora el?   ....

     nada de   ....

     ¿mañana de la tarde o la de? ....

     muchas gracias bien   ....

     tarde de la   ....

b. gracias bien   ....

     ¿dónde para?   ....

     ¿sale autobús qué hora a el? ....

     la noche a once las de   ....

     Valencia para   ....

3 On tape you will hear the phone numbers of a city's principal offices being given. These are listed below; can you fill in their telephone numbers in the spaces provided? Answers on p. 90.

OFICINA DE TURISMO ....

CORREOS ....

RENFE ....

4 Next on tape you'll hear a number of train announcements. Listen carefully to where the trains come from and then fill in their times of arrival, in figures only, and platform numbers in the timetable below. Listen right through at least once before you try to write anything. Answers on p. 90.
(**el**) **andén** platform.

	Procedencia	Llegada	Anden
a.	SALAMANCA		
b.	VALENCIA		
c.	MADRID		
d.	LA CORUÑA		
e.	VIGO		
f.	BURGOS		

Grammar

Este, ese, aquel this, that, that one over there

Este means 'this' and changes according to the word it describes

este señor this man   **esta señora** this woman
estos niños these boys   **estas niñas** these girls

As you will have seen **este** can be used on its own to mean 'this one'
¿quién es éste? in dialogue 8 or 'these ones'. If used in this way, **éste** has
an accent.

In Spanish there are two words for 'that' **ese** (that one close to you) and
aquel (that one over there) so that if the item under discussion is close by,
you should use **ese** and if it's further away use **aquel**. **Ese** and **aquel** must
agree with the words they describe and change their endings accordingly

ese señor that man   **esa señora** that woman
esos autobuses those buses   **esas españolas** those Spanish
girls

aquel hombre that man   **aquella francesa** that French
girl
aquellos coches those cars   **aquellas niñas** those girls

24-hour clock

Here you simply translate both hours and minutes into their numerical
equivalents.

el autobús sale a las quince veintitres the bus leaves at 15:23
el tren llega a las dieciséis cuarenta the train arrives at 16:40

Days of the week and months of the year

Note that you don't need capital letters for either the days of the week or
the months of the year in Spanish.
Use **el** in front of the day of the week if you mean a particular day

llega <u>el</u> lunes he's coming on Monday

and **los** in front of the day of the week if it applies regularly to that day of
the week

siempre viene los lunes he always comes on Monday
trabaja los viernes she works on Friday (i.e. she regularly works
on Fridays)

If you are talking about dates, also use **el**

mi cumpleaños es *el* veintinueve de junio my birthday is the
29th of June
el tres de agosto . . . on the 3rd of August . . .

Read and understand

Study the bus timetable below and see if you can answer the questions. Answers on p. 90.

New vocabulary
(el) itinerario bus route
(la) gasolinera petrol station
(el) horario timetable
(la) primera salida first bus

(la) última salida last bus
(la) salida departure
cada every, each
(la) frecuencia frequency

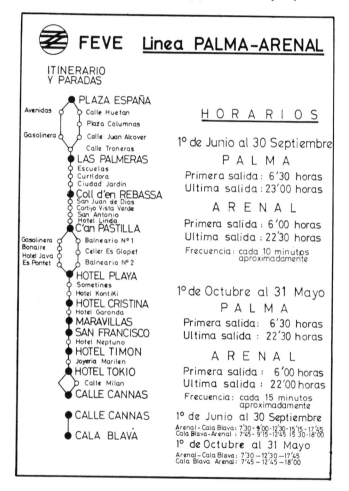

1. Is the timetable the same all the year round? ....

2. What is the earliest time that the bus leaves from Palma? from Arenal? ....

3. How frequently does it run in summer/winter? ....

Did you know?

The telephone service

You can make telephone calls in three different ways. Perhaps the easiest is to make a call through your hotel, but they will charge you for this service.

Alternatively, you could go to **La Telefónica** the telephone exchange (which is what Pepe did in this unit). Note that in Spain the telephone network operates independently of the post office, so don't expect to find phones in post offices! In large towns, telephone exchanges are open twenty-four hours a day, and here the operator will put your call through and give you the bill afterwards. Just write down the town and number you want on a piece of paper and hand it over to the operator. Add **de persona a persona** if you want a person-to-person call and **a cobro revertido** if you want to reverse the charges.

You can also phone from public telephones but make sure you are in a box marked **internacional**. If you need any help you can dial 008, the international information service. In Spain there is no central emergency service phone number; instead the various emergency services numbers are given in local newspapers or listed in telephone booths.

Buses

There are essentially two sorts of buses – the **coches de línea** which operate between large towns (book in advance) and the urban buses. Some large towns, like Madrid, operate **micro** buses – these are more expensive but a good deal less crowded than the ordinary buses. Bus timetables are available but it is probably easier to enquire at the hotel reception desk or simply ask a passer-by. On buses and subways there is a flat rate irrespective of distance and it is cheaper to buy a **taco** (a book of tickets) for underground travel. Subways operate between 6:00 a.m. and 1:00 a.m.

Your turn to speak

Now it's your turn to ask for information on timetables. Once you've read the instructions to the exercise, try not to consult your book, unless you really have to. Don't forget to use the pause button whenever you need a little extra time to think.

You're at the railway station and you want to ask the girl at the information desk about train times.

Answers

Revision p. 77 diez, catorce, veinticuatro, veintidós, quince, nueve, cinco, veintiocho, treinta y uno, diez y siete, diez y nueve, veintiún.

Practice what you have learned p. 85 Exercise 1 (a) las ocho (b) las diez cuarenta (c) la una (d) las quince horas quince minutos (e) las diecinueve cuarenta.

p. 86 **Exercise 3** Oficina de Turismo tel: 720777; Correos tel: 711580; Renfe tel: 712510.

p. 86 **Exercise 4** (a) 17.05 andén 2 (b) 18.45 andén 4
(c) 19.45 andén 2 (d) 20.45 andén 5 (e) 22.00 andén 4 (f) 23.35 andén 5.

Read and understand p. 88 (1) no (2) 6.30/6.00 (3) every ten minutes/ every fifteen minutes.

7 Shopping – part 1

What you will learn

- asking for certain items
- specifying exactly what you want
- asking what something costs
- saying that you don't want anything else
- understanding what the shopkeeper asks you
- something about food shopping in Spain
- weights and measures in Spain

Before you begin

There is a lot of new vocabulary to be learnt in this unit, all of it useful on a Spanish holiday. Learn it as thoroughly as you can now; you may not remember it all so come back to this unit later and revise it – particularly if you are planning a holiday in Spain.

Do you remember what the following foods are? (Answers p. 104)

el jamón ....

el helado ....

el queso ....

la naranja ....

los calamares fritos ....

Study guide

	Dialogues 1 – 3: listen straight through without the book
	Dialogues 1 – 3: listen, read and study one by one
	Dialogues 4 – 5: listen straight through without the book
	Dialogues 4 – 5: listen, read and study one by one
	Study the *Key words and phrases*
	Do the exercises in *Practice what you have learned*
	Study *Grammar*
	Complete *Read and understand*
	Read *Did you know?*
	Do the tape exercise in *Your turn to speak*
	Finally, listen to all the dialogues again without the book

Dialogues

1 *Pepe is buying batteries for his recorder*

Pepe ¿Me da cinco pilas de . . .?
Chica ¿Pequeñas?
Pepe No, de las grandes . . . Sí. ¿Estas son mejores que éstas?
Chica Son iguales.
Pepe ¿Son iguales, no? Cinco por favor. ¿Cuánto es todo?
Chica Ciento cincuenta y cuatro.

igual the same

2 *Buying milk and oil*

Pepe ¿Cuánto cuesta la leche por favor?
Tendero La leche, setenta y cinco pesetas litro y medio y cuarenta y cinco un litro.
Pepe ¿Tiene botellas de litro? ¿Y de medio litro no tiene?
Tendero No, de medio litro no hay.
Pepe De medio litro no. Y las botellas de aceite, ¿de qué tamaño son?
Tendero De litro o de dos litros.
Pepe ¿No tiene (no tiene) de medio litro?
Tendero No, de medio litro tampoco lo hacen ya.
Pepe ¿Y es aceite de oliva o aceite vegetal?
Tendero Hay aceite de oliva, aceite de girasol y aceite de maíz.
Pepe ¿Cuál es el más caro?
Tendero El más caro, el de oliva.

(el) tendero shopkeeper
(la) leche milk
(el) aceite oil
(el) olivo olive
(el) maíz corn
vegetal vegetable
(el) girasol sunflower

1 ♦ **¿me da cinco pilas de . . .?** can you give me five batteries?
You can also simply say:
♦ **cinco pilas por favor** five batteries please.

¿éstas son mejores que éstas? are these batteries better than these? More about **mejor** on p. 101.

♦ **¿cuánto es todo?** how much is everything?

2 ♦ **setenta y cinco pesetas litro y medio y cuarenta y cinco un litro** seventy-five pesetas for a litre and a half and forty-five for a litre. The metric system is used in Spain and so of course milk is sold by the litre. More about metric measurements in *Grammar*.

♦ **¿tiene botellas de litro?** have you got litre bottles? You've already learned two different ways of asking for items in dialogue 1. Here is another you should learn **¿tiene . . .?** do you have . . .? **¿tiene pilas?** do you have (i.e. stock) batteries?

♦ **¿de qué tamaño son?** what size are they? Size in clothing is **talla ¿qué talla es usted?** what size are you? but in shoes you must use **número ¿qué número es usted?** what size (shoe) are you? More about this in Unit 8.

no, de medio litro tampoco lo hacen ya no, they no longer make half-litre bottles either; **tampoco** = neither.

aceite de oliva, aceite de girasol y aceite de maíz olive oil, sunflower oil and corn oil. Spaniards cook mainly with oil so obviously they are keenly interested in the different varieties and qualities available.

♦ **¿cuál es el más caro?** which is the most expensive? **el más barato** the cheapest.

	3	*At the grocery store*

Marisa ¿Cuánto es la Coca-Cola pequeña? (Doce pesetas.) Vale. Tres
botellas de leche. Un litro de aceite.
Tendero Ciento cuarenta pesetas.
Marisa Una lata de aceitunas negras
Tendero Treinta y nueve pesetas.
Marisa Una docena de huevos. Doscientos gramos de mortadela. ¿A cómo
e(s) la mortadela?
Tendero Veintidós pesetas. Cuarenta y cuatro pesetas.
Marisa Vale.
Marisa Una bolsa de patatas fritas.
Tendero Cuarenta pesetas.
Marisa Y un paquete de sal gorda.

pequeño small
♦ **(la) lata** tin
(la) aceituna olive
negro black
♦ **(la) docena** dozen
♦ **(la) bolsa** bag
(la) patata frita crisp
♦ **(el) paquete** packet

	4	*Buying souvenirs*

Roldán Buenos días.
Luisa Buenos días, señor, ¿qué desea?
Roldán Quiero comprar algo de recuerdo, pero . . .
Luisa ¿Desea algo típico?
Roldán Sí.
Luisa ¿Qué le parece este plato?
Roldán Pues es demasiado grande ¿no? ¿No tiene más . . . otro más
pequeño?
Luisa Sí, éstos.
Roldán ¿Cuánto cuestan?
Luisa Cuatrocientas pesetas.
Roldán ¡Uy, qué caro! ¡Cuatrocientas pesetas! ¡Eso es carísimo!
Luisa Pero están muy bien hechos. No son caros.
Roldán Pues . . . ¿y éstos son los mas pequeños que hacen?
Luisa Sí, éstos son los más pequeños y esos los más grandes.

Luisa Muy bien, son setecientas pesetas. ¿Quiere algo más?
Roldán Sí, ¡pero no me queda dinero! ¿Tiene cambio de mil?
Luisa Sí, señor. Cien, doscientas, trescientas y las mil.
Roldán Muchas gracias.

demasiado grande too big

3   **una docena de huevos** a dozen eggs.

♦ **doscientos gramos de mortadela** two hundred grammes of mortadela (a mild Italian salami). 200g is roughly just under ½lb and is therefore a useful weight to know when buying cheeses and cold meats.

¿a cómo e(s) la mortadela? how much (is) the mortadela?

sal gorda coarse salt. **Gordo** usually means big or fat
un hombre gordo a fat man.

4 ♦ **quiero comprar algo de recuerdo** I want to buy something as a souvenir. **Un recuerdo** a souvenir, **recordar** to remember. If you are not quite sure what you want **quiero comprar algo** . . . I'd like to buy something . . . will come in very useful.

♦ **¿desea algo típico?** do you want something traditional? **típico** traditional or typically Spanish – a mantilla or castanets for example.

¿qué le parece este plato? what do you think of this plate? Ceramics is a popular craft throughout Spain.

¡uy, qué caro! ooh, how expensive! **qué + adjective** means how . . .!
¡qué inteligente! how intelligent! how clever! **¡qué interesante!** how interesting!

¡eso es carísimo! that's very expensive!

están muy bien hechos they are very well made.

¿y éstos son los más pequeños que hacen? and are these the smallest ones they make?

♦ **¿quiere algo más?** do you want anything else? You must be able to understand this as it's frequently asked by shopkeepers at the end of a sale. If you don't want anything say **nada más** nothing else.

♦ **¿tiene cambio de mil?** can you change a thousand pesetas (note)? **¿tiene cambio?** have you got change?

5 *Buying a suitcase*

Mari Buenas tardes, ¿puedo atenderle?
Pepe Sí por favor. Una maleta. ¿Puede decirme cuál es la mejor?
Mari ¿La prefiere en tipo bolso o maleta maleta?
Pepe (Um . . . tipo) maleta maleta.
Mari Maleta. Pues mire, tiene ésta, ésta es buena.
Pepe ¿Cuánto cuesta la más barata?
Mari Dos mil setenta y cinco.
Pepe (Dos mil) ¿También de cuero?
Mari No, ésta es de polipiel, imitación a piel.
Pepe Imitación a piel ¿y son duras?
Mari Sí, y además que están rebajada(s), están muy bien de precio.

(la) maleta suitcase
barata cheap
duro hard, strong

5

¿puede decirme cuál es la mejor? can you tell me which is the best?

¿puedo atenderle? can I help you? A more polite way of saying **¿desea algo?** do you want something?

¿la prefiere en tipo bolso o maleta? are you looking for a travelling bag or a proper suitcase?

pues mire well look. **Mirar** to look is a regular -**ar** verb.

ésta es de polipiel, imitación a piel this is made from 'polipiel', an imitation leather.

además que están rebajadas and besides, they're reduced . . . Look out for **Rebajas** (reductions, sales) in adverts and in shop windows if you're looking for a sale item.

están muy bien de precio they are at a very good price.

Key words and phrases

¿puedo atenderle?	can I help you?
¿desea algo?	do you want something?
¿me da (cinco pilas) por favor?	can you give me (five batteries) please?
quiero comprar (cinco pilas)	I want to buy (five batteries)
¿tiene (botellas de . . .)?	do you have (bottles of . . .)?
sí, (cuarenta y cinco) el litro	yes, (forty-five) pesetas a litre
¿de qué tamaño es?	what size is it?
¿cuál es . . .	which is . . .
el más caro?	the most expensive?
el más barato?	the cheapest?
¿(quiere) algo más?	(do you want) anything else?
sí, (doscientos gramos) de mortadela	yes, (200g) of mortadela
nada más	nothing else
¿cuánto es (todo)?	how much is (everything)?
¿tiene cambio de . . .?	do you have change for . . .?
¿desea algo típico?	would you like something typically Spanish?

Measurements

un litro de	a litre of
medio litro de	half a litre of
un litro y medio de	a litre and a half of
una botella de	a bottle of
un kilo de	a kilo of
medio kilo de	half a kilo of
doscientos gramos de	two hundred grammes of
una lata de	a tin of
una docena de	a dozen (of)
una bolsa de	a bag of
un paquete de	a packet of

Practice what you have learned

1 On tape you will hear a customer asking for various goods in a shop. If you hear any of the items pictured below being mentioned, tick the appropriate boxes. Answers on p. 104.

New vocabulary: **una barra de pan** a loaf of bread

2 Below you will see a sales slip with the number of items bought and their cost – but the names of each item is missing. Can you fill it in after you've listened to the dialogue on tape? Answers on p. 104.

New vocabulary: **(el) sombrero** hat   **(la) cantidad** quantity

EL CORTE INGLÉS

CANTIDAD	PRECIO
2	700 ptas
3	1·500 ptas
1	3·000 ptas
1	250 ptas

3 Listen to the list on your tape once or twice and then switch it off and see if you can match up the correct item in each column with a line.

un kilo	*de leche*
tres botellas	*de mortadela*
una docena	*de cerveza*
una barra	*de tomates*
un paquete	*de pan*
dos latas	*de patatas fritas*
500 gramos	*de sal*
seis botellines	*de sardinas*
una bolsa	*de huevos*

How much did it all cost?
Answers on p. 104.

4 On tape you will hear a conversation between a saleslady and a customer who is rather difficult to please. The transcript still has some omissions. Can you listen to the dialogue and then fill in the missing phrases?

New vocabulary: (**el**) **color** colour **burdeos** maroon **marrón** brown

Chica Buenas tardes. ¿Puedo atenderle?

Señora Sí, un .... por favor.

Chica Bien – ¿qué .... quiere?

Señora Un sombrero .... por favor ¿los tiene de . . .?

Chica Lo siento, de .... no tenemos. Mire tenemos

.... son grandes y los hay en varios

....

Señora ¿Qué .... tiene?

Chica ...., verde y ....

Señora ¿No .... de otros colores?

Chica No, de otros .... no.

Señora ¿Cuánto ....?

Chica Estos – pues mil ....

Señora Uy, ¡qué ....

Chica No, señora .... están rebajados.

Señora ¿No tiene más ....? .... de

allí, ¿cuánto ....?

Chica .... mil .... pero los

tenemos sólo en ....

Señora ¿En marrón? Pues no. Muchas .... señorita.

Chica A ....

Grammar

Comparatives

In English you can qualify adjectives by putting *more* or *most* in front of them e.g. *more beautiful, most beautiful.* You can also use special forms e.g. *nice, nicer, nicest.* In Spanish it is much easier as most adjectives are qualified by putting 'more' **más** or 'most' **el más** in front of them.

caro (a, os, as)	expensive
más caro (a, os, as)	more expensive
el más caro	the most expensive (masc. sing.)
la más cara	the most expensive (fem. sing.)
los más caros	the most expensive (masc. pl.)
las más caras	the most expensive (fem. pl.)

You can also use:

bastante caro (a, os, as)	quite expensive
demasiado caro (a, os, as)	too expensive

You also need to know these special comparative words:

bien well
peor (es) worse
bueno (a, os, as) good
igual (es) the same
mejor (es) better
Estas pilas son buenas, pero ¿son mejores o peores que ésas?
These batteries are good, but are they better or worse than those?

Hacer to make or to do

hago I make/do	**hacemos** we make/do
haces you make/do	**hacéis** you make/do
hace he/she/it/you makes/does	**hacen** they/you make/do

hecho made/done
hecho a mano hand-made

Read and understand

Read the following passage and then answer the questions below (tick the correct boxes). Answers on p. 104.

Las islas Canarias son el paraíso del 'shopping'. Whisky, tabaco, cámaras fotográficas o de cine, magnetófonos, transistores – todo es más barato que en sus países de origen. Desde una piel de cocodrilo de Nigeria, hasta el marfil tallado o la auténtica seda china; aquí se pueden encontrar los objetos más raros.

Y en las islas Baleares también hay tradición y mercado de artesanía: las perlas artificiales, la cerámica, los zapatos hechos a mano. En Mahón se pueden comprar muy buenos zapatos a precios muy razonables. Las perlas son famosas en Manacor y Felanitx. Menorca tiene una brillante tradición de hacer muebles y platos típicos.

New vocabulary:
(la) **isla** island
(el) **paraíso** paradise
(el) **país** country
(el) **magnetófono** tape recorder
(el) **marfil tallado** carved ivory
(la) **seda** silk
(el) **zapato** shoes
(el) **cocodrilo** crocodile

a. What can you buy from China in the Canary islands?

☐ silk

☐ whisky

☐ shoes

b. Manacor specializes in ☐ embroidery

☐ pearls

☐ glass

c. Menorca has a tradition of furniture making ☐ yes

☐ no

d. Photographic equipment is less expensive in the Canary islands than in the manufacturing country ☐ yes

☐ no

e. Crocodile skins come from ☐ China

☐ Nigeria

☐ Mallorca

Did you know?

Metric measurements

Here are a few conversions in case you're not quite attuned yet!

1 kilo = 2.2lb
½ kilo = 1.1lb
1 litre = 1.76 pints
1 metre = 1.09 yds
1 km = 0.62 miles

Food shopping

If you are preparing your own meals, these are signs to look for: **Tienda de ultramarinos** (grocery) **Mantequería** (delicatessen), **Fiambres** (cold meat, cold cuts) **Carnicería** (butcher's), **Frutería** (fruit store) **Verdulería** (greengrocer's). However, if possible, buy fruit and vegetables in a market where they are usually cheaper and fresher than in the shops. Open-air markets are held once or twice a week in most Spanish towns and holiday resorts. Details about days and times may be obtained locally. Remember to take your own shopping bag as plastic bags etc. are not usually provided. You can of course pick and choose your own fruit and vegetables and the vendor will then weigh and price them for you.

Souvenirs

As there are so many crafts which are particular to certain areas, it's difficult to generalize about which things are the best buys. It's best to consult the local tourist office in the area you are visiting. In Madrid, you might enjoy a visit to the **Rastro**, a 'flea market'. Half of it is in the open air while the other half is housed in galleries around the market area and it sells anything and everything. It's particularly busy on Sundays when half of Madrid turns out to browse among the stalls. Steer clear of typical tourist shops and shop instead for your ceramics, leather goods etc. in the local markets where you can be sure of value for money.

Your turn to speak

1 You are at the grocer's buying provisions.

And finally Test yourself on the *Key words and phrases* and remember to play through all the dialogues again without looking at the book.

Answers

Revision p. 91 el jamón = ham, el helado = ice-cream, el queso = cheese, la naranja = orange, los calamares fritos = fried squid.

Practice what you have learned p. 98. Exercise 1 you should have ticked the following: the three tins of sardines, the dozen eggs, the loaf of bread, the six bottles of beer, the ham, the two tins of black olives, the coffee, the two bottles of milk, the cheese, the ice-cream.

p. 99 Exercise **2** platos, bolsos, maleta, sombrero.

p. 99 Exercise **3** un kilo de tomates, 500 gramos de mortadela, tres botellas de leche, dos latas de sardinas, un paquete de sal, una docena de huevos, seis botellines de cerveza, una bolsa de patatas fritas, una barra de pan. The total cost of these items was 810 pesetas.

p. 100 Exercise **4** the missing words were: sombrero; tipo; grande; cuero; cuero; éstos; colores; colores; burdeos; negro; tiene; colores; cuestan; quinientos; caros; además; baratos; ésos, cuestan; aquéllos; pesetas; marrón; gracias; usted.

Read and understand p. 102 (**a**) silk; (**b**) pearls; (**c**) yes; (**d**) yes; (**e**) Nigeria.

8 Shopping – part 2

What you will learn

- buying clothes and sports equipment
- paying with a credit card
- specifying colour and size
- asking for certain medicines
- something about drugstores
- something about opening and closing times

Before you begin

You will need to be able to give your size in Spanish so if you are still unsure about numbers in Spanish, go back now to Unit 4 and review the relevant section.

Study-tip   When you are doing odd jobs around the house, tune your radio to a Spanish station. You may not understand much of it to start with, but you will at least be listening to the rhythm and intonation of the language. As these become more familiar, you will find it easier to understand what people are saying in Spanish, and to have less of a foreign accent yourself.
    Remember these useful expressions for shopping:

quiero I'd like. . .
¿tiene. . .? do you have. . .?
nada más nothing else
¿cuánto es? how much is that?

Study guide

	Dialogues 1 – 4: listen straight through without the book
	Dialogues 1 – 4: listen, read and study one by one
	Dialogues 5 – 8: listen straight through without the book
	Dialogues 5 – 8: listen, read and study one by one
	Study the *Key words and phrases*
	Do the exercises in *Practice what you have learned*
	Study *Grammar*
	Complete *Read and understand*
	Read *Did you know?*
	Do the tape exercise in *Your turn to speak*
	Finally, listen to all the dialogues again without the book

Dialogues

1 Buying sports equipment

Pepe Oiga. ¿Venden ustedes artículos de deporte?
Dependiente Sí, sí. Los tenemos aquí en la planta baja.
Pepe ¿Venden ustedes cosas para tenis?
Dependiente Sí, sí, vestidos, pantalones, pelotas, raquetas, de todo, vamo(s) . . .
Pepe ¿Y venden ustedes también artículos para fútbol?
Dependiente Botas, medias, camisetas, pantalones, chandal, balones, todo, todo . . .
Pepe Bien, muchas gracias.
Dependiente De nada.

(**el**) **artículo** article
(**el**) **deporte** sport
(**la**) **cosa** thing
(**el**) **tenis** tennis
(**el**) **vestido** dress
(**la**) **pelota** ball (small)

(**la**) **raqueta** racket
(**el**) **fútbol** football, soccer
(**la**) **bota** boot
(**las**) **medias** stockings
(**la**) **camiseta** tee-shirt
(**el**) **chandal** track suit
(**el**) **balón** ball (large)

2 Buying a mantilla

Pepe Por favor, ¿venden ustedes mantillas aquí?
Rosa Sí, sí, mantilla(s), ¿como la(s) desea (eh), pequeñita(s) grande(s)?
Pepe ¿Cuánto cuestan las grandes?
Rosa Bueno, la(s) hay de varios tamaños. La(s) hay pequeñita(s), desde unas mil doscienta(s) peseta(s) hasta siete mil peseta(s).
Pepe ¿Y (cuán . . .) cuánto cuestan las más baratas?
Rosa Las más baratas sobre unas dos mil peseta(s), cinco mil peseta(s). . .
Pepe ¿Y son todas negras?
Rosa No, que la(s) tenemos negra(s), beige, azul, gris, dorada(s) plateada(s); la(s) tenemos también en colore(s) de varios tamaños, estampada(s). . .

pequeñitas small
azul blue
gris grey

doradas gold
plateadas silver
estampadas printed, patterned

3 Buying a headscarf

Pepe ¿Y venden ustedes pañuelos de cabeza?
Dependienta Sí, también tenemo(s) pañuelo(s) de cabeza.
Pepe ¿Y cuánto cuestan los más caros?
Dependienta Los caro(s) . . . de dos mil peseta(s).
Pepe Los pañuelos ¿de qué son? Los pañuelos de cabeza, ¿son todos de algodón o de . . .?
Dependienta No, lo(s) hay de algodón, de batista, de poliester, de crepe, de seda natural.
Pepe ¿Y cuáles son los más baratos?
Dependienta Lo(s) de poliester.

(**el**) **pañuelo de cabeza** headscarf
(**el**) **algodón** cotton
(**la**) **batista** batiste

(**el**) **poliester** polyester
crepe crepe
(**la**) **seda natural** natural silk

1 ◆ **¿venden ustedes?** do you sell?

de todo, vamos well, everything. **Vamos** comes from **ir** (to go) and is used here as a filler word.

2 **mantilla** the traditional lace scarf worn by Spanish women.

las hay de varios tamaños there are (mantillas) in various sizes. **Las** the, refers here to **las mantillas** – as you see, you don't have to keep repeating the noun. This is dealt with more fully on p. 115.

las más baratas sobre unas dos mil pesetas the cheapest are about two thousand pesetas. **Sobre** can mean 'about' – though its more common meaning is 'on': **sobre la mesa** = on the table.

3 **los de poliester** the polyester ones. **Los** here stands for headscarves (**los pañuelos de cabeza**).

4 *Asking for advice in a menswear department*

Jefe Buenas tardes.

Pepe Buenas tardes, por favor (um desea . . .) deseo comprar una chaqueta pero no sé qué tipo de chaqueta. ¿Podría aconsejarme?

Jefe Sí, ¿cómo no? Podríamos aconsejarle una chaqueta de cheviot, es propia de esta época. No es ni muy gruesa, ni es muy fina.

Pepe ¿Tiene de otros colores? Porque . . .

Jefe Tenemos varios tonos de color, como son los grises, los verdes, los marrones, o las clásicas blazers, azul marino.

Pepe ¿Cuánto cuesta ésta?

Jefe Estos tipos de chaquetas tienen varios precios, según calidades, y terminaciones, oscilan entre siete y once mil pesetas.

(el) jefe de sección head of department (in a store)
de cheviot lambswool from the Cheviot Hills which border England and Scotland
(el) tono shade
verde green
según according to
(la) calidad quality
(la) terminación finish
oscilan they vary

5 *And now Pepe is looking for some trousers to go with the jacket*

Jefe Buenas tardes, ¿en qué podemos serle útil?

Pepe Estoy buscando unos pantalones.

Jefe Sí, ¿para usted? ¿o es para . . ?

Pepe Sí, para mí . . .

Jefe Para usted. Vamos a tomar la medida por favor, para saber su talla. Sí. Cuarenta y dos . . .

Pepe (Um) ¿Qué tipo de pantalones tiene?

Jefe ¿Usted lo desea para ahora o lo prefiere para verano?

Pepe Para verano.

Jefe Para verano.

4 ◆ **deseo comprar una chaqueta** I want to buy a jacket.

¿podría aconsejarme? could you advise me? and the assistant replies **podríamos aconsejarle** we could advise you.

es propia de esta época it's right for this time of year.

no es ni muy gruesa, ni es muy fina it's neither too thick nor too thin. Note this use of **muy** = too. **ni . . . ni** = neither . . . nor.

las clásicas blazers, azul marino the classic blazers in navy blue. **Blazers** is of course borrowed from the English.

5 ◆ **¿en qué podemos serle útil?** how can we help you?

◆ **estoy buscando unos pantalones** I am looking for some trousers. If you are a woman you might like to learn **estoy buscando una falda** I am looking for a skirt.

vamos a tomar la medida por favor, para saber su talla let's measure you please, to find out your size. Pepe is a size 42. Find out what your size would be abroad (see the clothing chart on p. 117) and then practise asking for it **¿tiene la talla 38?**

◆ **usted lo desea para ahora o lo prefiere para verano?** do you want it for now or would you prefer it for summer? The other three seasons of the year are **(el) otoño** autumn; **(el) invierno** winter; **(la) primavera** spring.

6 *Paying for your purchases*

Pepe ¿Puedo pagar con tarjeta de banco por favor?

Jefe Por supuesto, cualquier tarjeta que sea de uso normal puede usted hacer su compra dentro de nuestro establecimiento.

Pepe ¿Puedo pagar con una tarjeta de banco inglés internacional?

Jefe Sí, sí, naturalmente, sí, sí.

Pepe Bien, muchas gracias.

Jefe A usted, señor.

7 *Looking for something a little different?*

Jefe Buenas tardes, señorita, ¿qué deseaba?

Victoria Pue(s) mire, he venido para comprarme un vestido, algo de fantasía . . . algo de novedad, no sé; algo distinto.

Jefe Quiere usted pasar por aquí, vamos a mostrarle . . .

Victoria Vale, yo me quedo con éste que me gusta. ¿Dónde puedo pasar a abonarla?

Jefe Pase usted aquí a caja por favor . . .

8 *At the chemist's/pharmacy*

Pepe ¿Tiene alguna medicina para el dolor de estómago por favor?

Farmacéutica Sí, sí ¿cómo lo quería, en comprimidos, jarabe? ¿qué es, para ardor de estómago, dolor, malas digestiones?

Pepe Es para malas digestiones.

Farmacéutica Malas digestiones. Pues sí, hay unos comprimidos Polidasa.

Pepe ¿Y tiene algún bronceador?

Farmacéutica Sí, bronceadores, sí.

(**la**) **farmacéutica** pharmacist (women)
(**el**) **comprimido** tablet
algún bronceador some suntan lotion

6 ♦ **¿puedo pagar con tarjeta de banco?** can I pay with a bank card? Pepe might have also asked **¿puedo pagar con cheques de viaje?** Can I pay with travellers' cheques? or **¿puedo pagar con tarjeta de crédito?** can I pay with a credit card?

cualquier tarjeta que sea de uso normal puede usted hacer su compra dentro de nuestro establecimiento (lit. whatever card which can be used ordinarily you can use to make your purchase in our store) you can use any ordinary (bank) card in our store. Here the **jefe** is speaking in an unusually formal manner.

7 **¿qué deseaba?** what did you want?

mire, he venido para comprarme un vestido, algo de fantasía look, I've come to buy a dress, something a bit different. Victoria uses a past tense **he venido** = have come which needn't worry you here – we shall be looking at past tenses in Unit 15.

algo de novedad, no sé; algo distinto something new, I don't know; something different.

quiere usted pasar por aquí, vamos a mostrarle . . . if you'd like to come this way, we can show you . . .

♦ **yo me quedo con éste, que me gusta** I'll have this one, I like it.

♦ **¿dónde puedo pasar a abonarla?** where do I go to pay (for it)? (This should be abonar**lo**, as it refers to **el vestido**.) And perhaps the more commonly heard **¿dónde puedo pagar?** and **¿dónde puedo pasar a pagar?** = where do I go to pay?

♦ **pase usted aquí a caja por favor** this way to the cashier please.

8 ♦ **¿tiene alguna medicina para el dolor de estómago?** have you any medicine for a stomach-ache?

¿cómo lo quería? how did you want it?

jarabe syrup; **jarabe para la tos** cough mixture in liquid form.

¿para ardor de estómago, dolor, malas digestiones? for heartburn, pain, indigestion?

Key words and phrases

¿en qué podemos serle útil? — how can we help you?
¿qué deseaba? — what did you want?

¿venden ustedes (artículos de deporte)? — do you sell (sports equipment)?
estoy buscando (unos pantalones) — I'm looking for (some trousers)
deseo comprar (una chaqueta) — I'd like to buy (a jacket)
¿qué tipo de (chaqueta) tiene? — what type of (jackets) do you have?
¿tiene la talla (cuarenta y dos)? — do you have size (42)?

¿tiene (algo, alguna medicina) para (el dolor de estómago)? — do you have (anything, any medicine) for (a stomach-ache)?

yo me quedo con (éste) — I'll take (this one)
¿puedo pagar con. . . — can I pay with. . .
   tarjeta de banco? — a bank card?
   cheques de viaje? — travellers' cheques?
   tarjeta de crédito? — a credit card
¿dónde puedo pagar? — where do I pay?
¿dónde puedo pasar a pagar? — where do I go to pay?
¿dónde puedo pasar a abonarlo? — where do I go to pay for it?
pase usted a la caja — go to the cashier
¿usted lo desea para ahora? — do you want it for now?

Practice what you have learned

1 On tape you will hear a conversation between a customer and a sales assistant. The customer has 10.000 pesetas to spend. What does she decide to buy? When you have listened to the dialogue, switch the tape off and then tick the appropriate boxes. Answers on p. 118.

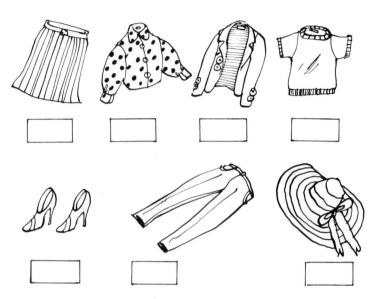

2 On tape you will hear two conversations. From these you should be able to tell which items the man enquired about and what his wife was interested in. Join up with a line the items in question with the husband/wife. Answers on p. 118.

3 On tape you will hear Carlos shopping. Listen to the conversation as many times as you like and then answer the questions below in English. Answers on p. 118.

a. What does Carlos want to buy?

....

b. What does he think his size is?

....

c. What shade of blue does he ask for?

....

d. How many types of material does the saleswoman offer him to start with?

....

e. What is wrong with the first garment he tries on?

....

f. What is wrong with the next one?

....

g. How much is the one he buys?

....

New vocabulary:
probar to try on

Grammar

Poder to be able

You have already learnt one part of this verb **se puede** (one can), **no se puede** (it is not allowed). If your memory needs refreshing turn back to the grammar section in Unit 5.

puedo	**podemos**
puedes	**podéis**
puede	**pueden**

(¿)puedo(?) I can/ can I(?)
(¿)puede(?) he can/can he(?) she can/can she(?) you can/can you(?)

It's always followed by an infinitive – the part of the verb that ends in **-ar** or **-er** or **-ir**.

¿y ahora puedo hacer la maleta? and now can I pack the suitcase?
¿puedo cambiar dinero aquí? can I change money here?

Infinitives follow lots of other verbs
quiero comprar un vestido I want to buy a dress
sé nadar I know how to swim

Saber and conocer

There are two verbs in Spanish for 'to know' and they are both irregular.

sé	**sabemos**	**conozco**	**conocemos**
sabes	**sabéis**	**conoces**	**conocéis**
sabe	**saben**	**conoce**	**conocen**

Use **saber** if you are talking about facts **lo sé** I know it, about languages **sé inglés** I know English and in the sense of knowing how to do something **sé nadar** I know how (can) to swim. Use **conocer** if you are talking about people **conoce a Pepe** he knows/is acquainted with Pepe or places **conozco Alemania** I know/am acquainted with Germany. Note that when you are talking about people you know you must use **conocer a**; **¿conoces a Luisa?** do you know Louise?

Direct object pronouns

You have already come across several examples of direct object pronouns in this unit: they are used simply to avoid repeating the name of the object in question **¿tiene la maleta?** do you have the suitcase? **no, no la tengo** no, I don't have it. In English we use *it* or *them* to refer to objects under discussion but in Spanish you use the word for *the* with the exception of **el** which changes to **lo** (remember that *the* has four forms).

¿quiere el libro? sí, lo quiero do you want the book? yes, I want it
¿quiere una mantilla? no, no la quiero do you want a mantilla? no, I don't want it
¿quiere unos pantalones? ¿los quiere de algodón? do you want some trousers? do you want them in cotton?
¿quieres aspirinas? sí, las quiero do you want aspirins? yes, I want them

The position of **lo, la, los, las** is usually just in front of the verb; where the verb is an infinitive, they are added on to the end.

voy a comprarlo I'm going to buy it
¿vas a tomarlas? are you going to take them?

Read and understand

FARMACIAS

Martes, 18 Noviembre
Farmacias abiertas de
1.30 a 4.30 tarde

Rubi Ponseti; Sindicato,
50. Tel. 212610.
Magdalena Salgado:
Isaac Albéniz, 16 (Son
Oliva). Tel. 297971.

Oliver Ferrer, José
Alemany Vich, 7 (Junto
Htas, de los Pobres)
(Bda. Gral Riera).
Tel. 291159.

Abiertas de 8 a 10 noche

Bernat Delteil: Colón,
18. Tel. 212173.

Calafell Clar:
Sindicato, 41.
Tel. 211446.
Cortes Cortes: Nuño
Sanz, 42 (Travesía
Balmes) Hostelets.
Tel. 273996

De 10 Noche a 9
Mañana

Miró Forteza: Colón,
6. Tel. 211368.

1 a. Tick the names of the pharmacies open from 1:30 – 4:30 p.m.

☐ Bernat Delteil
☐ Rubi Ponseti
☐ Miró Forteza

b. How many pharmacies are open all night? ....
c. When is Cortes Cortes open? ....
d. What is the phone number of Oliver Ferrer? ....

2 Read the following slip and then try filling in the necessary information.

New vocabulary:
rellene fill in
(**el**) **cupón** slip
envíelo send it
(**el**) **apartado de correos** box number
(**el**) **domicilio** residence

Si quiere tener una tarjeta de banco, rellene este
cupón y envíelo a Apartado de Correos 1, 245 Madrid

TARJETA DE CREDITO

Nombre   ....

Domicilio ....

....

Teléfono ....

Firma   ....

Answers on p. 118.

Did you know?

Clothing

Sizes differ between Spain and the U.S. The charts below should serve as a useful guide.

Men's clothes					
U.S.	36	38	40	42	44
Spain	46	48	50	52	54

Men's shirts				
U.S.	14	15	16	17
Spain	36	38	40	42

Women's clothes					
U.S.	12	14	16	18	20
Spain	40	42	44	46	48

Shoes									
U.S.	4½	5½	6½	7½	8½	9½	10½	11½	12½
Spain	35½	36½	38	39	41	42	43	44	45

Pharmacies and perfumeries

If you need drugs or medical advice you should go to a **farmacia**. You will find that many more medicines are available in Spain without prescription than over here. If you need a pharmacist at night, the local newspaper will carry a list of **farmacias de guardia** (these are the pharmacies whose turn it is to stay open – all pharmacies operate on a rota system). Despite its name you cannot buy drugs in a **droguería**: it's a hardware shop where you can buy soap, detergent and so on. Finally, as their name suggests **perfumerías** specialize in perfumes and scents.

Opening and closing times

Most shops close at lunch-time. Opening hours are usually 9/10:00. – 13:00/13:30 and then 15:00/15:30 – 19:30/20:00. However, check locally as times will vary according to the season and the area.

Your turn to speak

You are in the sports department of a large store. On tape Isabel will suggest what you should say to the sales assistant.

Answers

Practice what you have learned p. 113 Exercise 1 the woman bought: a skirt, a blouse and a jacket

p. 113 Exercise 2 the man was interested in a pair of trousers, a jacket and a pair of shoes and the woman in a tee-shirt, a blouse and a hat.

p. 114 Exercise 3 (a) a pair of trousers (b) 46 (c) navy blue (d) three (e) they're too small (f) they're the wrong colour (g) 5,600 pesetas.

Read and understand p. 116 Exercise 1 (a) Rubi Ponseti (b) one (c) from 8 – 10 at night (d) 291159

p. 116 Exercise 2 You should have filled in your name, your address, your telephone number and finally you should have signed the form.

9 Making travel arrangements

What you will learn

- hailing taxis
- specifying where you want to go
- understanding questions about your travel requirements
- asking for single and return tickets
- asking for gasoline and getting your oil and tires checked
- getting a puncture repaired
- some useful information about taxis and the railways
- and information about petrol stations in general

Before you begin

If you can, make your own travel arrangements, as you will have far more independence and flexibility on your holiday. It is also so much easier if you have to change your plans because of illness or strikes at airports. Travel arrangements necessarily involve times and dates, so you may find it helpful to review Unit 6 before going on with this unit.

Study guide

	Dialogues 1 – 4: listen straight through without the book
	Dialogues 1 – 4: listen, read and study one by one
	Dialogues 5 – 6: listen straight through without the book
	Dialogues 5 – 6: listen, read and study one by one
	Learn the *Key words and phrases*
	Do the exercises in *Practice what you have learned*
	Study *Grammar* and do the exercise
	Complete *Read and understand*
	Read *Did you know?*
	Do the tape exercise in *Your turn to speak*
	Finally, listen to all the dialogues again

Dialogues

1 *How do you get to school?*

Pepe	¿Se puede ir en autobús hasta tu colegio?
Javier	Sí, si tu lo prefiere(s).
Pepe	¿Está muy lejos tu colegio?
Javier	No.
Pepe	¿Cuán lejos está tu colegio?
Javier	A uno(s) cien metro(s).

2 *Hailing a taxi*

Pepe	Taxi, ¿queda libre?
Taxista	Sí, señor, ¿para dónde? ¿Para dónde va Vd.?
Pepe	Al ayuntamiento, por favor.
Taxista	Muy bien.
Taxista	Ya hemos llegado.
Pepe	Estupendo. ¿Cuánto es?
Taxista	Cien pesetas justas.

3 *Hailing another taxi*

Pepe	Taxi, taxi, ¿está libre?
Taxista	Sí, señor. ¿Adónde va Vd.?
Pepe	A la catedral por favor.
Taxista	Muy bien.
Taxista	Esta es la catedral.
Pepe	Gracias. ¿Cuánto le debo?
Taxista	Ciento veinticinco pesetas.

1 ♦ **¿se puede ir en autobús hasta tu colegio?** can you get to your school by bus? **¿se puede ir en coche?** can you go by car? **¿se puede ir en tren?** can you go by train? See *Key words and phrases* for further examples.

¿cuán lejos está tu colegio? how far is your school? **Cuán** is a shortened form of **cuánto** how much but it is an antiquated form and is not much used. **¿Cuán lejos está . . .?** how far is it . . .. ?

2 ♦ **taxi, ¿queda libre?** taxi, are you free? You can also use **¿está libre?** are you free? as Pepe does in dialogue 3.

♦ **¿para dónde?** where to? Answer this question with a phrase beginning **a** = to:
♦ **al ayuntamiento** to the town hall **a la catedral** to the cathedral **al aeropuerto** to the airport.

ya hemos llegado we have arrived, **ya** = already.

cien pesetas justas one hundred pesetas exactly.

3 ♦ **¿cuánto le debo?** how much do I owe you?

4 *At the gasoline station*

Pepe	Oiga, ¿tiene extra?
Gasolinero	No, tenemos sólo super o normal.
Pepe	Bueno, pues . . .
Gasolinero	¿Quiere que lo rellene?
Pepe	No, sólo quince li . . . no, veinte litros de super, por favor.
Gasolinero	Sí, claro, aquí tiene, veinte litros de super. ¿Quiere que le mire el nivel del aceite?
Pepe	No, gracias, no es necesario.
Gasolinero	¿Y quiere que compruebe la presión de las ruedas?
Pepe	Sí, las ruedas, sí, por favor, especialmente las dos de delante.
Gasolinero	Vale. ¿Quiere que le limpie el parabrisas?
Pepe	Sí, sí, porque está muy, muy, muy sucio, sí.
Gasolinero	De acuerdo. Ahora se lo haré.

necesario necessary
sucio dirty
de acuerdo all right, OK

5 *Repairing a tire*

Pepe	Oiga, ¿pueden repararme Vds. una rueda? que no llevo rueda de repuesto.
Gasolinero	De acuerdo, entonces ¿la necesita para ahora mismo?
Pepe	Sí, sería conveniente, porque no me gusta viajar sin rueda de repuesto.
Gasolinero	Bien, ¿puede esperar como un cuarto de hora o así?
Pepe	Sí, si es sólo cuestión de un cuarto de hora, sí, pues si es más, pues me voy y vuelvo dentro de un rato.
Gasolinero	No, no, será como un cuarto de hora o media hora.
Pepe	Estupendo, muy bien. Entonces espero. Ahora mismo . . . ¿dejo el coche aquí o lo llevo un poco más adelante?
Gasolinero	No, puede dejarlo allí mismo.
Pepe	Bien, bueno, estupendo.
Gasolinero	Vale.

(la) rueda de repuesto spare tire
necesita you need
así so
(la) cuestión question
será it will be
estupendo great
dejarlo leave it
allí mismo right there

4 **¿tiene extra? no, sólo super o normal** do you have extra? no, only super or regular. Extra, super and regular are the three grades of petrol normally available in Spain – more about this on p. 75.

¿quiere que lo rellene? would you like me to fill her up? **rellenar** to fill up.

♦ **veinte litros de super** twenty litres of super. You usually ask for petrol by the litre: **diez litros de** . . . ten litres of . . .

¿quiere que le mire el nivel del aceite? would you like me to look at/check the oil level? **nivel** = level.

¿quiere que compruebe la presión de las ruedas? would you like me to check the pressure of the tires?

especialmente las dos de delante especially the two at the front. **Las dos de atrás** = the two at the back.

¿quiere que le limpie el parabrisas? would you like me to clean the windshield?

ahora se lo haré I'll do it for you now; **haré** I will do.

5 ♦ **¿pueden repararme Vds. una rueda?** can you repair a wheel for me? Should anything else need repairing simply substitute the name of the object for **rueda**.
¿pueden repararme Vds. este reloj? can you repair this watch for me?

ahora mismo right now. More about **mismo** on p. 129.

sí, sería conveniente yes, that would be a good idea.
conveniente advisable/desirable.

no me gusta viajar sin rueda de repuesto I don't like travelling without a spare wheel. **(el) viaje** journey, voyage.

me voy y vuelvo dentro de un rato I'll go off and come back later. **dentro de un rato** (lit.) within a short time.

¿lo llevo un poco más adelante? shall I move it on a bit further?

6 *Buying a train ticket*

Pepe	Por favor, un billete para Madrid.
Dependiente	¿Para qué día lo desea?
Pepe	Para mañana.
Dependiente	Mañana, ¿a qué hora quiere usted salir?
Pepe	¿Por la noche es posible?
Dependiente	Sí, por la noche tiene usted uno a las once de la noche.
Pepe	Bueno, ése (ése) sirve.
Dependiente	¿En qué clase le doy, ¿qué clase desea, primera o segunda?
Pepe	¿Cuánto cuesta? ¿Cuál es la diferencia?
Dependiente	Aproximadamente unas seiscientas pesetas. Dos mil doscientas en primera y mil seiscientas diez en segunda.
Pepe	Bueno, en segunda por favor.
Dependiente	En segunda. ¿Ida y vuelta quiere Vd.?
Pepe	No, sólo ida, sólo ida.
Dependiente	¿Sólo ida, no? Son mil seiscientas diez pesetas.
Pepe	Bien.
Dependiente	¿Tiene usted diez pesetas suelta(s)? Muy bien, gracias.
Pepe	Adiós.
Dependiente	Adió(s).

salir to leave
(la) diferencia difference
posible possible

6 ◆ **un billete para Madrid** a ticket to Madrid.

¿para qué día lo desea? what day do you want it for?

para mañana for tomorrow. You've already met one of **mañana**'s meanings – morning: it can also mean tomorrow. So tomorrow morning = **mañana por la mañana** and tomorrow afternoon/evening = **mañana por la tarde**.

bueno, ése sí sirve yes, that one's all right.

¿en qué clase le doy? , **¿qué clas desea, primera o segunda?** what class shall I give you? what class do you want, first or second? You will need to reply **primera/segunda clase por favor** first/second class please.

¿ida y vuelta quiere usted? do you want a return? You should reply
◆ **un billete de ida y vuelta por favor** a return ticket please, or if you only want a single
◆ **sólo ida** or **ida solamente** a single only.

¿tiene usted diez pesetas sueltas? have you got ten pesetas? (in change).

RENFE HORARIO

SALIDAS

HORA	MINUTOS	CLASE de TREN	DESTINO	COCHES	OBSERVACIONES
7 3	7	TRANVIA	CORDOBA	2ª	
9 1	5	RAPIDO TER	SEVILLA S.B.	1ª-2ª	(1)
9 3	0	SEMIDIRECTO	MADRID	1ª-2ª BAR	
1 3 4	7	TRANVIA	CORDOBA	2ª	(1)
1 5 2	1	RAPIDO TALGO	MADRID	1ª-2ª BAR	
1 7 1	5	EXPRESO	BARCELONA	1ª-2ª BAR	
1 8 3	5	RAPIDO TER	CORDOBA	1ª-2ª	(2)
1 8 5	2	TRANVIA	PUENTE GENIL	2ª	(3)
1 9 5	0	TRANVIA	ALORA	2ª	
2 2 0	0	COSTA DEL SOL EXPRESO	MADRID	1ª-2ª	

LLEGADAS

HORA	MINUTOS	CLASE de TREN	PROCEDENCIA	COCHES
8 5	3	TRANVIA	ALORA	2
8 2	0	COSTA DEL SOL EXPRESO	MADRID	1ª-2
9 2	6	TRANVIA	PUENTE GENIL	2
1 1 3	0	RAPIDO TER	CORDOBA	2
1 2 4	5	EXPRESO	BARCELONA	1ª-2
1 5 0	0	TRANVIA	CORDOBA	2
1 6 3	9	TRANVIA	CORDOBA	2
2 0 4	2	SEMIDIRECTO	MADRID	1ª-2
2 1 0	4	RAPIDO TER	SEVILLA S.B.	1ª-2

Key words and phrases

¿cuán lejos está (la catedral)?	how far is (the cathedral)?
¿se puede ir . . .	can you go . . .
en autobús?	by bus?
en coche?	by car?
en tren?	by train
a pie?	on foot?
en bicicleta?	by bicycle?

Taxi

¿queda libre?	are you free?
al (ayuntamiento) por favor	to the (town hall) please
a (la catedral) por favor	to (the cathedral) please
¿cuánto le debo?	how much do I owe you?

Service station

¿tiene extra?	do you have 'extra'?
no, sólo super/normal	no, only 'super' or 'normal'
(veinte) litros de super	(twenty) litres of super
¿pueden repararme . . .	can you repair . . . for me?
una rueda?	a wheel
el coche?	the car

Railway station

un billete para (Madrid) por favor	a ticket to (Madrid) please
en (primera, segunda) clase	in (first/second) class
un billete de ida y vuelta	a return ticket
ida solamente	a single only

Practice what you have learned

1 Here's a muddled conversation. Can you unravel it? It's all about hailing a taxi. Write out the sentences in their correct order and then check your answers on p. 132.

Elena   ¿libre taxi queda? ....

Taxista   ¿dónde para sí? ....

Elena   por estación la a favor ....

Taxista   ésta estación la es ....

Elena   ¿cuánto le gracias debo? ....

Taxista   Cincuenta pesetas ciento ....

Elena   aquí bien tiene lo. ....

2 Here's a crossword for you to complete. All the answers are to be found in this unit and the clues are on the tape. The first letter of each answer has been filled in to help you. Answers on p. 132

New vocabulary:
horizontales clues across **verticales** clues down

3 Here's one side of a dialogue between you and a gasoline station attendant. The pictures will guide you as to what to write. Answers on p. 132.

¿Sí, señora?

Oiga ¿ .... ?

Lo siento, sólo tenemos super o normal.

Bueno ....

¿Miro el aceite?

....

¿Limpio el parabrisas?

Sí, ...

¿Compruebo la presión de las ruedas?

Sí, ...

Bien, buen viaje.

....

4 First of all listen to the tape. You will hear four short dialogues. Tick the grid below accordingly to each traveller's requirements.

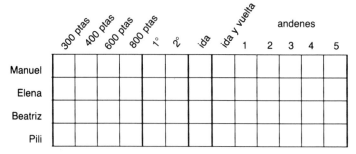

	300 ptas	400 ptas	600 ptas	800 ptas	1°	2°	ida	ida y vuelta	andenes 1	2	3	4	5
Manuel													
Elena													
Beatriz													
Pili													

Grammar

ir to go

If **ir** has a pronoun in front of it (e.g. **me, te, se**,etc) then the verb means
to go away or to go off: **voy** I'm going   **me voy** I'm going away.

(me)	voy	(nos)	vamos
(te)	vas	(os)	vaís
(se)	va	(se)	van

Mismo

This word can be translated in three different ways

1 **yo mismo** I myself
  tú mismo you yourself
2 **allí mismo** right there
  aquí mismo right here
  ahora mismo right now
3 **la misma señora** the same lady
  el mismo coche the same car
  (Note that in these cases **mismo** comes before the word it refers to
  and also agrees with it)

1 Fill in the blanks in the following sentences with **mismo/misma**. Answers
on p. 132.

a. Trabajo en la .... oficina.

b. ¡Ahora .... señor!

c. Está allí ....

d. Vivimos en la .... casa.

e. Yo .... la veo desde aquí.

My, your, his . . .
mi or **mis** my
mi mujer my wife, **mis hijos** my children
tu or **tus** your (familiar)
tu amigo your friend **tus zapatos** your shoes
su or **sus** his, her, their, your (formal)
nuestro, nuestra, nuestros, nuestras our
nuestro libro our book   **nuestros colegios** our schools
vuestro, vuestra, vuestros, vuestras your (familiar plural)
vuestra tarjeta de banco your bank card
vuestras naranjas your oranges

In this unit Pepe asks Javier

¿está lejos tu colegio? is your school far?

and Javier might have replied

no, voy andando a <u>mi</u> colegio no, I walk to school

And do you remember in Unit 8, the shop assistant telling Pepe

**cualquier tarjeta que sea de uso normal puede usted hacer <u>su</u>
compra dentro de <u>nuestro</u> establecimiento**

Read and understand

Read this notice and then tick the correct answers in the exercise that follows. Answers on p. 132.

FERROCARRILES
OFICINA

Servicio diario con Madrid, directos: duración, dos horas y veinte minutos.

Servicio de larga distancia con Palencia, Santander, Zamora, Orense, Vigo, León y Valladolid. Servicios combinados con el resto de las capitales.

La estación está situada en las afueras de Segovia, en la carretera de Villacastín. Autobús a la estación, media hora antes de la salida de cada tren. Salida de la Plaza de Franco, 8.

New vocabulary:
diario daily
(la) duración length
larga long

servicios combinados con services linking
(las) afueras outskirts

1 Trains leave for Madrid
- [ ] daily
- [ ] twice weekly
- [ ] on Sundays only

2 The journey to Madrid takes
- [ ] 2 hours 30 minutes
- [ ] 2 hours 20 minutes
- [ ] 3 hours

3 There's a long distance service to
- [ ] Valencia
- [ ] Palencia
- [ ] Santiago

4 The station is
- [ ] on the outskirts of Segovia
- [ ] in the middle of Segovia
- [ ] on the road to Estebanuela

5 There's a bus to the station
- [ ] quarter of an hour before departure
- [ ] an hour before departure
- [ ] half an hour before departure

Did you know?

Taxis

City taxis have meters and they begin at a fixed charge with the charge increasing per kilometre (fifteen pesetas per kilometre for instance). If you're going beyond the city limits or on a special excursion then negotiate the price beforehand – and remember that taxi drivers expect a tip – about 10% will do. There are lots of taxis in Madrid – they are black sedan cars with a red horizontal line. They display a green light at night and during the day a sign on the windshield which says **libre** (free) if they are available. Minicabs (**microtaxis**) are blue with a yellow line. Remember you'll be charged extra for luggage and beware of taxis that don't have these distinguishing marks – they will probably charge you exorbitant prices.

Railways

The name of the Spanish railways network is **RENFE** (**Red Nacional de Ferrocarriles Españoles**) and it organizes a bewildering number of train services. **Renfe**'s showpiece is the **Talgo** a luxury train for which a supplement is payable. (Fares are calculated according to the distance involved and then supplements are added for travel on the **Talgo**, **Electrotrén** and the **Ter**.) These last two trains are both fast and comfortable the only difference being the former is an electric train and the latter a diesel train. If we continue down this hierarchy of trains, next come the **Rápido** and the **Expreso**. Do not be misled by their names as these are both slow trains, the only difference being the first travels by night and the second by day! Last in this list are the short distance local trains which are not particularly reliable and which go under a variety of names: **Taf, Ferrobús, Omnibús, Tranvía, Automotor**.

Children travel free up to the age of three and pay half-price up to the age of seven. However, if you have an international ticket, children can travel free up to the age of four and travel half-price up to the age of twelve. On certain dates throughout the year known as **Días Azules** (Blue Days), numerous reductions are available on train travel; check with the Spanish Tourist Office for dates and further information.

Tariffs have been fixed per item of luggage for railway porters and they are obliged to carry a list of these tariffs. If you think you are being overcharged ask to see the list. (This also applies to airport porters.)

Your turn to speak

You are in a service station and you need to buy some petrol. Isabel will tell you exactly what to say.

And finally As usual, play through all the dialogues again. Then imagine you have to take a train from Barcelona to Madrid, and a taxi to the airport. Use the phrases you have learnt to arrange the journey.

Answers

Practice what you have learned p. 127 Exercise 1 Taxi, ¿queda libre?/Sí ¿para dónde?/A la estación, por favor/ Esta es la estación/Gracias, ¿cuánto le debo?/Ciento cincuenta pesetas/ Bien, aquí lo tiene/

p. 127 Exercise 2 *across* (**1**) colegio. (**2**) coche. (**3**) catedral. (**4**) rueda. *down* (**1**) normal. (**2**) bicicleta (**3**) veinte.

p. 128 Exercise 3 ¿Sí, señora?/Oiga ¿tiene extra?/Lo siento, sólo tenemos super o normal./Bueno, veinticinco litros de super por favor./¿Miro el aceite?/Sí, por favor./¿Limpio el parabrisas?/Sí, está muy sucio./ ¿Compruebo la presión de las ruedas?/Sí, las dos de delante./Bien, buen viaje./Gracias, adiós.

p. 128 Exercise 4 Manuel – primera clase/ida y vuelta/ andén dos/ ochocientas pesetas. Elena – segunda clase/ ida/ andén uno/ trescientas pesetas. Beatriz – segunda clase/ ida/andén tres/cuatrocientas pesetas. Pili – primera clase/ida y vuelta/ andén cuatro/ seiscientas pesetas.

Grammar p. 129 Exercise 1 (**a**) trabajo en la misma oficina (**b**) ¡ahora mismo señor! (**c**) está allí mismo (**d**) vivimos en la misma casa (**e**) yo mismo la veo desde aquí.

Read and understand p. 130 (**1**) daily (**2**) two hours twenty minutes (**3**) Palencia (**4**) outskirts of Segovia (**5**) half an hour before departure.

10 Food and drink

What you will learn

- asking for the menu
- asking for information about items on the menu
- ordering food
- asking about restaurants and the food they serve
- something about Spanish food and drink

Study guide

	Dialogues 1 – 2: listen straight through without the book
	Dialogues 1 – 2: listen, read and study one by one
	Dialogues 4 – 6: listen straight through without the book
	Dialogues 4 – 6: listen, read and study one by one
	Learn the *Key words and phrases*
	Do the exercises in *Practice what you have learned*
	Study *Grammar* and do the exercise
	Complete *Read and understand*
	Read *Did you know?*
	Do the tape exercise in *Your turn to speak*
	Listen to all the dialogues again and test yourself on *Key phrases*
	Do the revision/review exercises on p. 219

Dialogues

◻ **1** *Asking about local restaurants*

Pepe   Oiga, ¿hay un restaurante típico por aquí cerca?
Carmen   Sí, hay varios. Aquí en el pueblo y otros por la playa.
Pepe   ¿Cuál me recomienda?
Carmen   Pues está el Mesón Gallego que tiene bastante (bastante) comida y variedad.
Pepe   ¿Qué tipos, qué tipos de comida sirven allí?
Carmen   Pues tiene cocina regional, platos combinados.
Pepe   ¿(eh) Es caro o barato?
Carmen   No sé, pero ni caro ni barato, pero conozco otro que es bastante barato, si quiere ir.
Pepe   ¿Es un autoservicio o un restaurante normal?
Carmen   Es un restaurante normal de un tenedor pero cocinan muy bien.

sirven they serve
(el) tenedor fork
cocinan they cook

◻ **2** *The 'tenedor' system is explained*

Pepe   ¿Qué significa 'de un tenedor'?
Carmen   Pue(s) un tenedor es la categoría, según sea mejor o peor. Tienen un tenedor, dos, tres, según.
Pepe   Ah bien, y mientras más tenedores, mejor categoría, ¿no?
Carmen   Exactamente.
Pepe   ¿Y la comida es buena en un tenedor?
Carmen   Sí es buena, aquí es bastante buena.
Pepe   Bien, muchas gracias.
Carmen   De nada.

según according to, that depends

1   **en el pueblo y otros por la playa** in the village and others (restaurants) near the beach.

♦ **¿cuál me recomienda?** which do you recommend? **¿cuál me recomienda el azul o el rojo?** which do you recommend, the blue one or the red one?

♦ **¿qué me recomienda?** what do you recommend? **¿qué me recomienda, la sopa o el pescado?** what do you recommend, the soup or the fish?

el Mesón Gallego the name of a restaurant. **Mesón** = inn; however, the word is frequently used these days to conjure up an 'olde worlde' atmosphere and is applied to quite modern hotels and restaurants.

Gallego Galician.

tiene cocina regional, platos combinados they have regional dishes and one course meals. A **plato combinado** is a new invention – used to satisfy foreign demands but becoming increasingly popular with fast-food restaurants. It will usually consist of a vegetable, eggs and a cut of meat often served on toast.

¿es un autoservicio o es un restaurante normal? is it a self-service or an ordinary restaurant?

2   **un tenedor es la categoría, según sea mejor o peor** a fork denotes the category, depending on how good or bad it is.

y mientras más tenedores, mejor categoría and the more forks it has, the better it is. 'Forks' are awarded to restaurants in the same way that 'stars' are awarded to hotels. If you enjoy eating well, you may have use of this phrase **¿cuántos tenedores tiene el restaurante?** how many 'forks' does the restaurant have?

3 *Ordering the first course. (You'll find the menu – with English translations on p. 140)*

Camarero	Buenas tardes.
Friends	Buenas tardes, buenas tardes.
Camarero	¿Van a comer a la carta?
Antonio	Sí, por favor.
Luisa	¿Nos da el menú?
Camarero	Aquí tiene.
Luisa	A ver.
Camarero	Vamos a ver. ¿Qué van a tomar de primer plato?
Luisa	Consomé con huevo para mí.
Camarero	Consomé con huevo.
Luisa	Sí.
Antonio	Y para mí, entremeses.
Camarero	Entremeses.
Pepe	Y para mí también.
Camarero	Dos entremeses – ¿y para Vd.?
Pablo	(Eh) sopa del día . . . Oiga, ¿qué es la sopa del día?
Camarero	Sopa del día, me parece que es sopa de pescado.
Pablo	Muy bien

(el) pescado fish

4 *The main course*

Camarero	¿Y de segundo plato?
Pepe	Para mí. . . mm. . . sí para mí, ternera a la riojana.
Luisa	Yo prefiero merluza a la romana.
Pablo	¿Y hay bacalao a la vizcaína?
Camarero	Pues sí, me parece que sí.
Pablo	Bien.
Antonio	Y para mí, señor, cochinillo asado, oiga, ¿es muy picante?
Camarero	Muy picante, no, no.
Antonio	Bueno, está bien.

picante spicy
(dulce sweet)

3   ¿van a comer a la carta? are you going to eat 'à la carte'? as opposed to having the set menu **el menú a precio fijo.**

♦ **¿nos da el menú?** may we have the menu?

¿qué van a tomar de primer plato? what will you have for first course? You will need to know

♦ **de primer plato, la sopa** for first course, the soup
♦ and similarly **de segundo plato** . . . for second course . . .
♦ and **de postre** . . . for dessert. . .

sopa del día soup of the day

♦ **me parece que es** I think it's. Also note **me parece que sí** I think so and **me parece que no** I don't think so. **Me parece bien** that seems like a good idea.

ESPECIALIDADES

CALAMARES

DORADAS

GAMBAS

LENGUADOS

MEJILLONES

MERLUZAS

5 *And the dessert*

Camarero	Y de postre ¿qué desean?
Pepe	No sé . . . ¿qué?
Luisa	¿Qué queréis tomar?
Pablo	Un flan.
Camarero	Un flan, sí, sí . . .
Camarero	Tenemos flan, tarta helada, melocotón.
Luisa	Sí, sí. (fruta) Para mí tarta helada.
Pepe	Y para mí también, tarta helada por favor . . . y tú, Antonio, ¿qué quieres?
Antonio	¿Hay helado, hay helado?
Camarero	Sí.
Antonio	Bueno, ¿qué hay? ¿fresa?
Camarero	Pues hay fresa, vainilla y chocolate.
Antonio	Vale, vale, de fresa.
Pepe	Y tú, ¿tú has pedido?
Luisa	Sí, un flan.
Camarero	O sea, son dos tartas heladas, un helado.
Pepe	De fresa.
Antonio	De fresa y un flan.
Pepe	Sí.

(la) fruta fruit   **o sea** that is to say
fría cold

6 *Ordering drinks*

Camarero	¿Algo más, algo más? (¿y para beber?) ¿para beber?
Luisa	¿Para beber, que tiene de beber? ¿Vinos . . .?
Camarero	Tenemos vino tinto, vino blanco, de la casa y también de marca.
Luisa	Pues yo creo que sería mejor una botella de vino tinto.
Camarero	¿De la casa?
Luisa	Sí, sí, de la casa.
Camarero	¿Una garrafa, una garrafa?
Pepe	¿De qué tamaño(s) son, de litro, de medio litro?
Camarero	Pue(s) de litro y también de medio litro.
Pepe	¿Una botella, una garrafa de litro para todos? ¿Vale?
Luisa	Sí, sí, sí.
Antonio	¿Y hay agua mineral?
Camarero	También. ¿Con gas o sin gas?
Antonio	Con gas.
Camarero	Con gas.
Pablo	Sí, sí. Para mí también.
Pepe	Sí, OK vale, vale, traiga Vd. una botella de agua mineral con gas – no – ¿hemos dicho con gas? Con gas y (luego) una garrafa de litro y si se acaba, pedimo(s) má(s) no?
Pablo	Sí, sí, sí . . . Estupendo.
Pepe	Vale.

(la) garrafa carafe
traiga bring

5   **y tú, ¿tú has pedido?** and you, have you ordered?

6 ◆   **¿qué tiene de beber?** what do you have to drink? **¿qué tiene de comer?** what do you have to eat?

vino tinto, vino blanco, de la casa y también de marca red wine, white wine, house wine and also branded varieties

pues yo creo que sería mejor una botella de vino tinto well I think a bottle of red wine would be best.

¿y hay agua mineral? and is there mineral water? Remember that it comes **con gas** or **sin gas** – fizzy or still – **¿hemos dicho con gas?** did we say 'fizzy'?

y si se acaba, pedimos más ¿no? and if it runs out, we'll ask for some more, shall we?

Key words and phrases

¿me da el menú?	can I have the menu?
¿nos da el menú?	can we have the menu?
¿qué tiene de beber?	what do you have to drink?
¿qué tiene de comer?	what do you have to eat?
de primer plato	as a first course
de segundo plato	as a second course
de postre	as a dessert
¿qué me recomienda?	what do you recommend?
¿cuál me recomienda?	which do you recommend?
me parece que sí	I think so
me parece que no	I don't think so
me parece bien	that seems a good idea
me parece que es . . .	I think it's . . .

MESON GALLEGO
Menú del día

Primer grupo	**First course**
sopa del día	soup of the day
(sopa de pescado)	(- fish soup)
consomé con huevo	consomé with egg
entremeses	hors d'œuvres
Segundo grupo	**Second course**
ternera a la riojana	Riojan veal
merluza a la romana	hake fried in batter
bacalao a la vizcaína	Vizcayan salt cod
cochinillo asado	roast suckling pig
Postres	**Desserts**
flan	cream caramel
tarta helada	ice-cream gateau
helados (fresa, vainilla, chocolate, caramelo)	ice-creams (strawberry, vanilla, chocolate, caramel)
melocotón	peach
vino tinto / blanco de la casa	red / white house wine

Practice what you have learned

1   On the tape you will hear Miguel and Eloisa discussing various restaurants. Listen to the dialogue and then draw lines between the restaurants below and their appropriate 'fork' categories. Answers on p. 146.

2   Listen now to a couple ordering a meal from the menu opposite. Who chooses what? Link the right person with the item on the menu by drawing a line between them. Answers on p. 146.

3 Imagine you're a waiter taking orders in a restaurant. Listen to the dialogue on tape carefully and then fill in the chit below. Answers on p. 146.

....	....
....	....
....	....
....	....
....	....

4 In this exercise you're the customer. Choose the appropriate answers to the waiter's queries from the box below. Answers on p. 146

Camarero Buenas tardes señora, ¿qué desea?

Cliente ....

Camarero Sí, claro.

Cliente ....

Camarero Me parece que es sopa de pescado.

Cliente ....

Camarero ¿Y de segundo plato?

Cliente ....

Camarero Sí, sí, muy bueno.

Cliente ....

Camarero ¿Y de postre?

Cliente ....

Camarero Me parece que no – hay flan, helados.

Cliente ....

---

pues el bacalao a la vizcaína   ¿de qué es la sopa?   ¿hay tarta helada?

¿el bacalao es bueno?

¿me da el menú por favor?   bien, la sopa por favor

un helado, por favor

Grammar

Para mí

You've probably noticed that after **para** for, you must use **mí** me. The same is also true for the informal **tú** you: after **para**, you must use **tí**. ¿Y **para tí**? **Un helado de fresa, por favor.** And for you? A strawberry ice-cream, please. However, in the cases of the formal *you, us, they* and so on there is no change, which is why the waiter asked ¿**y para usted?** and for you? in dialogue 4. The special forms **mí** and **tí** are used after all prepositions i.e. those 'linking' words like **de** 'of ', **sin** 'without' and of course **para**.

One exception however is the preposition **con** 'with'. It has two special forms for 'with me' and 'with you' and they are:

conmigo with me
contigo with you

1 Answer the following questions in Spanish (Answers p. 146.)

a. ¿para quién es esto? (it's for me) ....

b. ¿es para mí? (no, it's for you) ....

c. ¿y tú vas conmigo? (yes, I'll come with you) ....

d. ¿y la tarta helada, es para Vd.? (yes, it's for me) ....

e. ¿y el pan, dónde está? (it's near me) ....

f. ¡uy! ¿y comes sin mí? (no, I'm not eating without you) ....

....

Ordinal numbers

primero first	**quinto** fifth	**noveno** ninth
segundo second	**sexto** sixth	**décimo** tenth
tercero third	**séptimo** seventh	
cuarto fourth	**octavo** eighth	

Note: **1** All ordinals are adjectives and therefore must agree with the noun they describe

la segunda naranja the second orange
el séptimo alumno the seventh pupil

2 **Primero** and **tercero** have irregular forms. When they come immediately before the word they refer to, these two ordinals lose their final **o**.

el tercer piso the third floor
el primer plato the first course

3 However, when the noun they agree with is feminine, both **primer** and **tercer** take a final **a**

la primera planta the first floor
la tercera casa the third house

Read and understand

Quesos españoles

El queso soluciona una mala comida y complementa una buena.
'Una buena comida sin queso es como una mujer que no tiene un
ojo' – dijo el francés Brillat Savarin. La verdad es que el queso
forma parte importante de una comida francesa pero no de una
comida española.

Quesos de oveja, de vaca y de cabra son los tres tipos generales:
diecisiete tipos de queso en el primer grupo, doce en el segundo y
siete en el tercero. Los quesos de oveja son mejores que los otros.
El más conocido de los quesos españoles es el manchego – tiene
una forma cilíndrica y es muy bueno con el vino de Valdepeñas,
blanco o tinto.

New vocabulary:
(los) quesos cheeses
soluciona solves the problem of
(el) ojo eye
dijo said

(la) oveja sheep
(la) vaca cow
(la) cabra goat
conocido known

True or false?

		Verdad	Mentira
1	Cheese forms an important part of a Spanish meal	☐	☐
2	There are three main types of cheese in Spain	☐	☐
3	The best known Spanish cheese is Cabrales	☐	☐
4	Valdepeñas is a good wine to accompany Manchego cheese	☐	☐
5	Manchego cheese is rectangular in shape	☐	☐
6	There are thirty-six varieties of Spanish cheese	☐	☐

Answers p. 146.

Did you know?

The dialogues in this unit and those in Unit 4 should have given you some idea about Spanish food and drink but let us now look a bit more closely at what is available.

Wines

Wines can be very good in Spain and those to be recommended include **Priorat** and **Rioja** (from the Ebro region in northern Spain). Andalusia produces some good dessert wines such as **Montilla** or **Moriles** which taste rather like sherry – though somewhat lighter – and which have a similar pale brown colour. **Vino de la casa** (house wine) is always cheaper than **vino de marca**. If you are a sherry drinker, you might enjoy a visit to Jerez de la Frontera in Andalusia where much of the sherry exported to the U.S. comes from. Spanish people (apart from Andalusians) are not great **jerez** drinkers and those who do drink it usually have it as a cold drink with ice cubes! If you are looking for a refreshing drink try **sangría** – a universally popular punch in Spain. The basic ingredients are iced red wine, lemonade, fruit and any of the following: brandy, rum, cointreau etc. Some of these mixtures can be quite lethal so be careful! If you want a non-alcoholic drink try a **granizado** – an iced drink available in a variety of flavours or an **horchata**, a cold drink made of tiger nuts, sugar and water.

Specialties

Most regions of course have their own particular specialities and you'd probably be best advised to ask the waiter what goes into each dish. You can be sure, however, that most dishes contain olive oil: this is what gives Spanish cooking its distinctive flavour. On a visit to Spain you should of course try some of the better known dishes such as **paella**. It can be found all over the country with slight variations, but the 'classic' paella comes from the Valencia region. The 'basic' ingredients are rice cooked with saffron, olive oil, chicken, lean pork, cured ham, eels, green peas, broad beans, French beans, freshwater crayfish, snails, artichokes, green peppers, garlic, onion, spices and aromatic herbs. This is a **paella valenciana** but you might also come across a **paella marinera** which, as the name implies, is a seafood paella. The Catalan region of Spain also produces its own paella which has spicy pork sausages, pork, squid, tomato, chilli pepper and peas.

Cheese

The most popular Spanish cheese is called **manchego** from La Mancha. It's a hard cheese which gets correspondingly better and more expensive as it ripens. You'll see a lot of goat's cheese on sale, **queso de cabra**, and the local varieties are usually very good. You might also try **queso de teta** a firm, bland cheese made from cow's milk or **queso de roncal**, a salted, smoked cheese made from ewe's milk.

Manners

By the way it is polite to say ¡**qué aproveche**! (lit. enjoy your meal!) to people eating at other tables in a restaurant. If you're eating in the company of others (on a bus or train for instance) you should offer your meal to other passengers saying '¿**usted gusta?**' They will of course refuse but they should reply '**gracias ¡qué aproveche!**'

Your turn to speak

You will be ordering some wine at the Mesón Gallego. Isabel will tell you what to choose.

And finally   Make sure you've understood everything and know the *Key phrases* by listening once more to all the dialogues before you start work on the *Revision* section.

Revision/Review

Now turn to p. 219 and complete the revision sections for Units 6–10. On the cassette the revision section follows straight after this unit.

Answers

Practice what you have learned p. 141 Exercise 1 El Colón: cuatro tenedores/El Mesón Fernando e Isabel: tres tenedores/ El Mesón Gallego: tres tenedores/La Cueva de Tía Juanita: dos tenedores/El Polo: un tenedor.

p. 141 Exercise 2 The man ordered: sopa del día; ternera a la riojana; garrafa de vino blanco. The woman ordered: entremeses; bacalao a la vizcaína; helado de naranja; agua mineral sin gas.

p. 142 Exercise 3 Un consomé/dos sopas del día/merluza/bacalao/cochinillo asado/helado de chocolate/flan/tarta helada/garrafa de vino tinto.

p. 142 Exercise 4 Buenas tardes señora ¿qué desea?/ ¿Me da el menú por favor?/ Sí, claro./ ¿De qué es la sopa?/ Me parece que es sopa de pescado./ Bien, la sopa por favor./ ¿Y de segundo plato?/ ¿El bacalao es bueno?/ Sí, sí, muy bueno./ Pues el bacalao a la vizcaína./ ¿Y de postre?/ ¿Hay tarta helada?/ Me parece que no – hay flan, helados . . ./ Un helado, por favor.

Grammar p. 143 Exercise 1 (**a**) es para mí (**b**) no, es para tí (**c**) sí, voy contigo (**d**) sí, es para mí (**e**) está cerca de mí (**f**) no, no como sin tí.

Read and understand p. 144 (**1**) mentira. (**2**) verdad. (**3**) mentira (**4**) verdad. (**5**) mentira. (**6**) verdad.

11 Likes and dislikes

What you will learn

- expressing your likes and dislikes
- talking more about where you live
- more vocabulary to do with food and drink
- something about bullfights and Spain's *ferias* and *fiestas*

Before you begin

As soon as you get on friendly terms with a Spanish person, you will find yourself wanting to express likes and dislikes. You will find the most common ways of doing so listed in *Key words and phrases*: learn these well as you will probably have to use them every day of your holiday.

Study guide

	Dialogues 1 – 3: listen straight through without your book
	Dialogues 1 – 3: listen, read and study one by one
	Dialogues 4 – 6: listen straight through without your book
	Dialogues 4 – 6: listen, read and study one by one
	Learn the *Key words and phrases*
	Do the exercises in *Practice what you have learned*
	Study *Grammar* and do the exercises
	Complete *Read and understand*
	Read *Did you know?*
	Do the tape exercise in *Your turn to speak*
	Listen to all the dialogues again and test yourself on the *Key words and phrases*

Dialogues

1 *Do you like housework?*

Pepe ¿Le gusta cocinar?
Janet Sí, no mucho, pero sí me gusta.
Pepe ¿Y le gusta coser?
Janet Sí, muchísimo.
Pepe ¿Le gusta planchar?
Janet No, no, no, no, lo odio.
Pepe ¿Le gusta lavar?
Janet Lavar, ¿en qué sentido? ¿Lavar ropa?
Pepe Lavar la ropa.
Janet No, es un trabajo duro.
Pepe ¿Le gusta limpiar la casa?
Janet Sí, sí, me gusta.
Pepe ¿Qué es lo que le gusta menos de la casa, del trabajo de la casa?
Janet Planchar.
Pepe Planchar. ¿Y qué es lo que le gusta más?
Janet Limpiar la casa.
Pepe Limpiar la casa, bien.

planchar to iron
lavar to wash
(la) ropa clothes
(el) trabajo work
duro hard

2 *Food and drink*

Serafín ¿Le gusta el vino?
Janet Sí, me encanta.
Serafín ¿Prefiere el vino o la cerveza?
Janet Prefiero el vino tinto.
Serafín ¿Qué tipo de comida prefiere?
Janet Bueno, carne o huevos o lechuga.
Serafín ¿Cómo prefiere la carne?
Janet Muy bien frita.
Serafín ¿Le gustan los huevos?
Janet Ah sí, muchísimo.

(la) carne meat
(la) lechuga lettuce

1 ◆ **¿le gusta cocinar?** do you like cooking? **¿le gusta viajar?** do you like travelling? and you should answer **me gusta** I like it or **sí, me gusta** yes, I like it. Note that any verb that follows **le gusta** or **me gusta** is in the infinitive.

¿le gusta coser? do you like sewing? If you want to reply that you very much like doing a particular thing say **sí, me gusta muchísimo** yes, I like it a lot.

◆ **lo odio** I hate it. It's equally important to be able to express dislikes and if you want to be emphatic repeat yourself **no, no, no, lo odio** no, no, no, I hate it.

¿en qué sentido? in what sense? **lavar** can be interpreted in two ways **lavar la ropa** to wash clothes and **lavarse** to wash oneself.

◆ **¿qué es lo que le gusta menos?** what is it that you like least? And the reply **lo que me gusta menos es viajar** what I least like doing is travelling or **lo que me gusta menos de la casa** . . . what I like least *about* the house.

◆ **¿y qué es lo que le gusta más de?** and what do you like most about? (**lo que** lit. that which). Similarly the reply to this question would be **lo que me gusta más de la casa** what I like most about the house.

2 **¿le gusta el vino?** do you like wine? Note that you don't always need a verb after **¿le gusta?** you can have a noun too. **¿le gusta el agua mineral?** do you like mineral water?

me encanta I like it very much (lit. it enchants me). Used very much in the same way as the English 'I love it.' Use either **me gusta muchísimo** or **me encanta** to express a real liking for something.

muy bien frita very thoroughly fried.

¿le gustan los huevos? do you like eggs? Note that because **huevos** is plural, **gusta** becomes **gustan**. **¿le gustan los vinos franceses?** do you like French wines? **¿le gustan las frutas?** do you like fruit?

3 *Does Janet like Spain?*

Serafín ¿Le gusta España?
Janet Sí, me gusta muchísimo.
Serafín ¿Le gusta viajar?
Janet Sí, también.
Serafín ¿Qué tal el clima aquí en invierno?
Janet Hace frío, pero no mucho.

4 *Which regions does she like?*

Serafín ¿Conoce Valencia?
Janet Ah sí, me encanta, es una ciudad preciosa.
Serafín ¿Conoce la Costa del Sol?
Janet No, la detesto, no me gusta nada, nada, nada.
Serafín ¿Por qué?
Janet Hay demasiada gente.
Serafín ¿Y la costa más al sur?
Janet No especialmente. No me gusta ni mucho ni poco. Prefiero la costa gallega.
Serafín ¿No le gusta el mediterráneo?
Janet No me hace mucha gracia.
Serafín Pero las playas del mediterráneo son estupendas.
Janet Sí, pero hay demasiada gente.

preciosa beautiful
(el) mediterráneo the Mediterranean
(las) playas beaches

Benidorm

3 ◆ **¿qué tal el clima aquí en invierno?** what's the climate like here in winter? You will remember that to ask people how they are feeling you use **¿qué tal?** how are you? The same expression can also be used to ask how things are **¿qué tal el vino?** what's the wine like? **¿qué tal las vacaciones?** how did the holidays go?

hace frío pero no mucho it's cold, but not very. Weather will be discussed in the next unit.

4 **la Costa del Sol** the sunshine coast. At the southernmost tip of Spain this coastline stretches from Tarifa to Almería and takes in some of the favourite tourist spots such as Torremolinos, Fuengirola, Málaga etc.

◆ **no, la detesto** no, I hate it. You've already met one verb for to hate in this unit, can you remember what it was? If not, look at the notes to dialogue 1 again.

◆ **no me gusta nada, nada, nada** I don't like it one bit. If you want to say you don't like something, simply put **no** in front of **me gusta; no me gusta el sol** I don't like the sun. Again note the repetition of the word **nada** for emphasis.

hay demasiada gente there are too many people. Note that **gente** is feminine and that, as in English, it is a singular.

◆ **no me gusta ni mucho ni poco** I don't like it or dislike it. If you're feeling indifferent this is the expression for you!

◆ **no me hace mucha gracia** I don't like it very much/I'm not all that keen on it.

5 *And what do Spaniards think of England?*

Pepe   ¿Qué más te gusta de Inglaterra? ¿Qué es lo que te gusta más de Inglaterra?

Maria Luisa   Pues realmente (eh) lo que más me gusta es el paisaje. Tiene un paisaje muy verde, unos valles y unos parques muy bonitos.

Pepe   ¿Y qué es lo que te gusta menos de Inglaterra?

Maria Luisa   (eh) La lengua. La encuentro un poquito difícil.

Pepe   ¿Es difícil el inglés?

Maria Luisa   Sí, sí, es difícil.

realmente really
(el) paisaje countryside
(el) valle valley
(el) parque park
bonito pleasant/nice
(la) lengua language
encuentro I find
difícil difficult

6 *Spanish men and household chores*

María Luisa   Vamos a ver que piensa el hombre español del trabajo doméstico. ¿Te gusta cocinar?

Juan   No, no, es un trabajo para mujeres.

María Luisa   ¿Pero entonces te gusta lavar o planchar?

Juan   No, eso menos. Todavía cocinar, si es para freír un par de huevos, pues sí, pero no lavar y planchar – de eso, nada. La cocina, planchar y lavar, eso son cosas de la casa. Eso es para la mujer. Ella se encarga de todo, ella plancha y yo, cuando necesito una camisa, que la tenga bien preparada.

María Luisa   Pero entonces, cuando tu mujer no puede trabajar en casa, tendrás que plancharte las camisas cuando ella sale a trabajar – ¿o no?

Juan   Bueno, pues ya la(s) planchará la vecina – si no – yo no voy a planchar las camisas.

María Luisa   Pero ¿por qué realmente no te gusta planchar camisas?

Juan   Pero es que tampoco sabemos planchar, yo creo que un español no (no) puede planchar camisas.

María Luisa   ¡Qué español más típico y qué animales!

piensa think
(el) trabajo doméstico housework
(la) mujer woman, wife
todavía still, yet
freír to fry
(el) par pair, couple
(la) cosa thing
(los) animales animals

5 **¿qué más te gusta de Inglaterra?** what do you like best about England?
Note that **¿te gusta?** has replaced **¿le gusta?** This is because María Luisa
is an old friend and Pepe therefore uses the less formal **tú**.

6 **pero no lavar y planchar – de eso, nada** but washing and ironing –
certainly not – I won't have anything to do with that.

ella se encarga de todo she looks after everything.

y cuando necesito una camisa, que la tenga bien preparada and when I
need a shirt, then she'd better have it ready.

tendrás que plancharte las camisas cuando ella sale a trabajar you'll
have to iron your own shirts when she goes out to work.

pues ya las planchará la vecina well the neighbour will have to iron them.

pero es que tampoco sabemos planchar but it's that we don't know how
to iron either.

Key words and phrases

me encanta (el clima)	I love (the climate)
me gusta (muchísimo)	I like (very much)
me gusta el vino muchísimo	I like wine very much
no me gusta	I don't like
no me gusta nada, nada, nada	I don't like (it) at all
no me gusta el mediterráneo	I don't like the Mediterranean
no me gusta ni mucho, ni poco	I don't care one way or the other
lo odio	I hate it
lo detesto	I hate it
lo que me gusta más es	what I like most is
lo que me gusta menos es	what I like least is
prefiero (el café)	I prefer (coffee)
no me hace mucha gracia	I don't like it very much/I'm not very keen about it
¿qué tal (el clima)?	what's (the climate) like?

Practice what you have learned

1 On tape you will hear a conversation between Miguel and Elena about her likes and dislikes. The illustrations below depict various household chores. Beneath each illustration, write down the expression she uses to describe her feelings about that particular task. Answers p. 160

New vocabulary:
hacer la cama to make the bed
hacer las maletas to pack suitcases

a. .... b. .... c. .... d. ....

....

e. .... f. .... g. .... h. ....

....

2 Listen to Isabel asking Beatriz and Tomás about their food preferences. If either of them like the foods below, fill in their names. Answers on p. 160

New vocabulary:
jamón serrano raw ham which has been cured in wood smoke.

a. .... b. .... c. .... d. ....

....

e. .... f. .... g. ....

....

3 On tape you'll hear Miguel and Rosario discussing some Spanish regions. Tick the appropriate box below according to whether Rosario likes the area a lot, is indifferent towards it, or dislikes it. Answers on p. 160.

	le gusta muchísimo	no le gusta ni mucho ni poco	la detesta
Andalucía			
la costa del sol			
la costa gallega			
Madrid			

4 On tape you will hear Antonio listing his likes and dislikes. Listen to what he has to say and then fill in the table below. Answers on p. 160.

Does Antonio like?	sí	no
vino blanco		
vino tinto		
café solo		
café con leche		
Madrid		
Valencia		
las vacaciones		
el trabajo		
el norte de España		
el sur de España		
helado de fresa		
helado de chocolate		
la carne		
el pescado		

Grammar

Two new verbs appeared in this unit and both mean 'to think'.

Pensar **pienso   pensamos**
piensas pensáis
piensa   piensan

Note that **pensar en** means to think about

pienso en mis vacaciones I'm thinking about my holidays

Creer This verb also means 'to think' though more in the sense of 'to believe'
Yo creo que un español no puede planchar camisas
I don't think (believe) a Spaniard can iron shirts

Creer que can also be used in the same way as **parecer que**
me parece que sí/creo que sí I think so
me parece que no/creo que no I think not

creo   creemos
crees creéis
cree   creen

1 Fill in the gaps with either **creer/pensar** or **creer que/pensar que**. Answers p. 160.

a. ¿Juan está aquí? .... sí.

b. .... una buena comida ¡paella, vino blanco y flan!

c. ¿Hay tarta helada? .... no.

Me gusta I like (lit. it pleases me)

me gusta I like it   **no me gusta** I don't like it
te gusta   **no te gusta**
le gusta   **no le gusta**
nos gusta   **no nos gusta**
os gusta   **no os gusta**
les gusta   **no les gusta**

Note If the thing you like or don't like is plural, then you must use **gustan**
no me gustan los huevos I don't like eggs
me gustan las flores I like flowers
It's worth remembering the pronouns **me, te, le** as they will be cropping up later – in fact, you've already had some examples in **me parece que sí** I think so; **me encanta** I love it

2 Columns A and B have got muddled up. Can you unravel the mix-up by drawing lines between the two columns? Answers p. 160.

A	B
me gustan	nada nada nada
¿le gusta	muchísimo
¿qué te gusta más	los huevos
no me gusta	el fútbol o el tenis?
me gusta	España?

Read and understand

La Costa del Sol es un paraíso mediterráneo con aguas azules y playas de gran extensión y unas montañas suaves. El clima mediterráneo es templado y sin grandes variaciones y visitantes de todos los países encuentran el descanso que da el ambiente relajante. La Costa del Sol se extiende desde Almería a Tarifa y es una región de gran variedad.

Cocina y vinos – esta costa tiene muchos productos de excelente calidad. Hay una enorme variedad de platos de pescado – atún, sardinas, mariscos . . . El plato más famoso es el gazpacho. Universalmente famoso es el vino de Málaga, de magnífico aroma.

New vocabulary:

suave soft	**se extiende** extends
templado moderate	**(la) calidad** quality
(el) descanso rest	**(el) atún** tuna
(el) ambiente atmosphere	**(los) mariscos** shellfish
relajante relaxing	**(el) gazpacho** a cold tomato/garlic soup

You won't need to use all these words yourself. This is the rather flowery language of a tourist brochure.

Tick the correct statement. Answers on p. 160.

1 On the Costa del Sol the climate is
  - [ ] **a.** very hot
  - [ ] **b.** moderate
  - [ ] **c.** hot in summer and cold in winter

2 Visitors come
  - [ ] **a.** to rest
  - [ ] **b.** to enjoy themselves
  - [ ] **c.** for the sporting activities

3 The Costa del Sol extends from
  - [ ] **a.** Almería to Tarifa
  - [ ] **b.** Granada to Almería
  - [ ] **c.** Málaga to Cádiz

4 The Costa del Sol is especially known for its
  - [ ] **a.** meat
  - [ ] **b.** fish
  - [ ] **c.** fruit

5 Especially renowned is the wine from
  - [ ] **a.** Málaga
  - [ ] **b.** Granada
  - [ ] **c.** Nerja

Did you know?

Bullfights

Over recent years bullfights have begun to lose some of their popularity but there are still plenty to be seen during the months of April – November. Bullfights or **corridas** take place throughout the length and breadth of Spain on most Sundays during the season. Even if you are unable to see a **corrida**, you will probably be able to catch a **novillada** when apprentice bullfighters are allowed to face young bulls. Tickets are sold according to whether you want a seat in the **sol** (sun) which is cheaper, or in the **sombra** (shade). As bullfights can last a few hours, you'd probably be wise to invest in a more expensive ticket and save yourself the agony of sunburn. If you see a sign which reads **no quedan localidades**, it means they've sold out of tickets. Ticket touts will probably be much in evidence: you will of course have to pay over the odds for a ticket but make sure it's not too expensive. The top ring is in Madrid, but there is a good season in Barcelona. And finally, bullfights are among the few events in Spain which begin on time, so arrive early.

Ferias and fiestas

The main events in the bullfighting calendar coincide with the **ferias** and **fiestas**, the annual fairs throughout Spain. Most Spanish towns and villages, no matter how small, have their own local **ferias**, each with a distinct character of its own. Some of them are so highly distinctive that they have been given the rating of Festivals of Tourist Interest.

The highlight of all **fiestas** in Spain is Holy Week and the celebrations in Andalucía are probably the most widely known outside Spain. The statues of saints, Jesus Christ and the Virgin Mary are taken out of their churches and paraded through the streets on floats to the accompaniment of **saetas** (prayers sung in the flamenco style). They are often escorted by groups of penitents who wear hoods to cover their faces and who will sometimes walk alongside the float carrying a cross or with a ball and chain attached to their ankles.

Three Spanish festivals are famous throughout the world: the **fallas** in Valencia, the April Fair in Seville and the **San Fermín** in Pamplona. The Valencia fair takes place in March and the highlight of the occasion is the burning of the huge wood or plaster groups of caricatures depicting topical scenes known as **fallas**.

The Seville fair is a celebration of music and dancing which lasts six days. During that time, **sevillanos** dress in traditional costume and parade through the streets on horseback. Hundreds of canvas tents are set up as temporary places for parties and rented by families for the duration of the **feria**. During the evenings most people are out **de paseo** (strolling about the city) and if you are lucky you might find yourself being invited into one of these tents to join in a party. There is little chance of getting to bed before 2 a.m. during the **feria**.

And finally, if you're in Spain in July, a visit to Pamplona for the **San Fermín** festivities is a must. There you can join the young men of the town running through the streets in front of the bulls which are to be fought that afternoon in the bullring. There are also all the usual ingredients of a Spanish **fiesta**: music, dancing, good food and wine.

Your turn to speak

In this exercise, you are being asked which areas of Spain you like and why. You'll be practising the phrases you have learnt to express likes and dislikes (see p. 154) and you will also need the 'geographical' vocabulary you have met (north, south, east, west, coast etc).

And finally   Listen to the dialogues again and test yourself on the *Key words and phrases*. Then give yourself some extra practice by seeing how many of your own likes and dislikes you can express in Spanish.

Answers

Practice what you have learned p. 155 Exercise 1 (**a**) no me hace mucha gracia (**b**) lo detesto (**c**) me gusta (**d**) no me gusta nada, nada, nada (**e**) no me gusta ni mucho ni poco (**f**) lo detesto (**g**) me gusta mucho (**h**) me encanta.

p. 155 Exercise 2 (**a**) Beatriz, Tomás (**b**) Beatriz (**c**) neither of them like ice-cream (**d**) Beatriz (**e**) Beatriz (**f**) Tomás (**g**) Tomás, Beatriz.

p. 156 Exercise 3 Andalucía – no le gusta ni mucho ni poco. La Costa del Sol – la detesta. La costa gallega – le gusta muchísimo. Madrid – le gusta muchísimo.

p. 156 Exercise 4 sí to: vino blanco, el café solo, Valencia, el trabajo, el norte de España, helado de chocolate, la carne; no to the rest.

Grammar p. 157 Exercise 1 (**a**) creo que sí (**b**) pienso en (**c**) creo que no

p. 157 Exercise 2 me gustan los huevos; ¿le gusta España?; ¿qué te gusta más, el fútbol o el tenis?; no me gusta nada, nada, nada; me gusta muchísimo.

Read and understand p. 158 (**1**) moderate (**2**) to rest (**3**) Almería to Tarifa (**4**) fish (**5**) Málaga

12 The weather

What you will learn

- asking about the weather
- describing the weather conditions in your country
- something about the climate in Spain and the Canaries
- something about the northern coast of Spain

Before you begin

Talking about the weather is a peculiarly British preoccupation, but it is useful to be able to ask about the weather forecast if you are planning to go sailing or skiing or walking. In Spain, of course, all temperatures will be given in centigrade but it's quite easy to convert centigrade into fahrenheit: simply divide by 5, multiply by 9 and add 32! Here are a few examples:

°F	°C	
98.4	36.9	body temperature
86	30	
77	25	
68	20	
59	15	
50	10	

In Spain you shouldn't need any temperatures below 10°!

Study guide

	Dialogues 1 – 5: listen straight through without the book
	Dialogues 1 – 5: listen, read and study one by one
	Dialogues 6 – 7: listen straight through without the book
	Dialogues 6 – 7: listen, read and study one by one
	Study the *Key words and phrases*
	Do the exercises in *Practice what you have learned*
	Study *Grammar* and do the exercise
	Complete *Read and understand*
	Read *Did you know?*
	Do the tape exercise in *Your turn to speak*
	Listen to all the dialogues again without the book

Dialogues

1 *The weather in Seville*

Rosario	¿Hace frío en invierno aquí?
Tere	Sí mucho, muchísimo.
Rosario	¿Hace calor aquí en verano?
Tere	Muchísimo, una barbaridad.
Rosario	¿Hace buen tiempo, estos días?
Tere	Estupendo.
Rosario	¿Qué tal el tiempo aquí?
Tere	Ahora bueno, agradable.

estos días these days
agradable agreeable

2 *Weather conditions generally*

Judy	¿Y cómo es el clima aquí?
Serafín	Pues bueno normalmente.
Judy	¿En el norte?
Serafín	En el norte bastante lluvioso.
Judy	¿En el sur?
Serafín	Más bien seco y caluroso.
Judy	¿En la costa mediterránea?
Serafín	Pues suave y caluroso también.
Judy	¿Y en el centro?
Serafín	Más bien extremo. En verano bastante caliente y en invierno, bastante frío.
Judy	¿Hace frío aquí en invierno?
Serafín	Pues sí, bastante frío aquí en el centro.
Judy	¿Y hace calor en verano?
Serafín	Mucho calor normalmente.

◆ **suave** mild
   (el) centro centre
◆ **extremo** extreme
   caliente hot
   (el) calor heat

1 ♦ **¿hace frío en invierno aquí?** is it cold here in winter? Note the use of the verb **hacer** to do/to make in many 'weather phrases': **hace sol** it's sunny.

una barbaridad (lit. a barbarity) a lot. You will find that Spaniards pepper their conversation with exclamations and the word **barbaridad** is more commonly used in the expression **¡qué barbaridad!** how awful!

♦ **¿hace buen tiempo?** is the weather good? Here is another example of the use of **hacer** in a weather expression. And in case the weather is bad use **no, hace mal tiempo. Tiempo** means both weather and time **¿qué tiempo tiene?** what time is it? (lit. what time do you have?) **todo el tiempo** all the time.

2 ♦ **¿y cómo es el clima aquí?** and what's the climate like here? Because you are talking about the climate, and using **(el) clima** there is no need to use the verb **hacer**. Similarly the answers do not rely on the use of **hacer**. So, if the person who puts the question uses **es**, reply using **es ¿es lluvioso aquí? sí, es lluvioso** and if they use **hace**, reply using **hace ¿hace calor? sí, hace calor.**

♦ **en el norte bastante lluvioso** in the north, quite rainy (*it's* is understood). **Lluvioso** is from **lluvia** rain.

♦ **más bien seco y caluroso** on the hot and dry side. **Seco** can be used to describe climatic conditions or types of wine **un vino seco** a dry wine; **caluroso** is from **calor** heat.

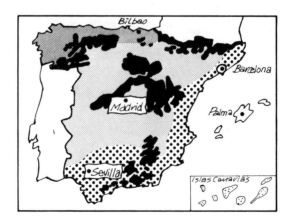

Continental climate

Atlantic climate

Mediterranean climate

Mountain ranges

3 *Another discussion on the weather*

Shade   ¿Qué tal aquí el clima en invierno?
Pedro   Bueno, depende de las regiones. (Y) Si está en la costa, pues bastante suave y si es en el centro, bastante frío, pero seco.
Shade   ¿Y en verano?
Pedro   Bueno en verano bastante caluroso, sobre todo en el centro y en la costa pues bastante suave con la brisa del mar. Y ¿en su país?
Shade   Hace bastante frío, pero, claro, depende de la región también.

sobre todo above all
(la) brisa breeze
(el) país country
(el) mar the sea

4 *Where Rosa lives, the climate is dreadful!*

Pepe   ¿Qué tal el clima en su país?
Rosa   Prefiero no hablar del tiempo en mi país.
Pepe   ¿Es malo?
Rosa   ¡Malísimo!
Pepe   Pues, en esta parte del país es una primavera eterna.

(la) primavera spring
eterna eternal

5 *Roy goes to Spain to escape the English weather*

Pepe   ¿Vienen siempre en verano?
Roy   (pues) Normalmente, pero a veces también venimos en primavera, en otoño y más de una vez durante el invierno.
Pepe   ¿En invierno hace frío aquí?
Roy   No, ¡qué va! No, ¡qué va – (eh) no tanto como en mi país y llueve mucho menos.
Pepe   ¿Y llueve mucho en su país?
Roy   Todo el tiempo, en invierno, en otoño, en primavera y en verano.
Pepe   ¿En verano llueve?
Roy   ¡Hombre, claro!
Pepe   ¡Vaya! pues lo siento, hombre, lo siento.

siempre always
a veces at times
más de una vez more than once

3   **¿y en verano?** Shade actually says **verana** here. Pedro understands and corrects her mistake in his answer. You'll find you don't need to worry if you make small mistakes like this when you talk. People will still understand you.

♦ **bueno, depende de las regiones** well, it depends on the regions. You should have no trouble remembering this useful verb as it's so like its English counterpart!

4 ♦ **pues, en esta parte del país es una primavera eterna** well, in this part of the country it's eternally springtime. The Costa del Sol has a mild and pleasant climate throughout the year and this is one of its main attractions to tourists.

5   **no ¡qué va!** no, what rubbish! what nonsense! One of the many phrases in which the verb **ir** is used. There is another example later on in this dialogue **¡vaya!** well, I say!

no tanto como en mi país y llueve mucho menos not as much as in my country and it rains a good deal less. If you're asked to describe the English weather, you'll probably need: (**el**) **viento** wind, (**la**) **nieve** snow, **nevar** to snow, (**la**) **niebla** fog and above all **nubloso** cloudy and **cubierto** overcast. **¿hace viento?** is it windy? **no, hay niebla hoy** no, it's foggy today.

6 *High season prices*

Pepe ¿Qué significa 'temporada alta' por favor?

Señorita La temporada alta son los mese(s) que más turismo hay en la ciudad. Por ejemplo . . . no entonces . . . si.
No, le quiero decir que entonce(s) hay uno(s) precio(s) establecido(s) que – (um) o sea, hay un período (un período) de sesenta día(s) al año que el hotel puede hacer un recargo de un quince por ciento. Entonce(s) el hotel tiene que especificarlo en (en) recepción. Tiene que decírselo al cliente que se está cobrando el quince por ciento por ser la temporada alta.

Pepe Entonces, en temporada alta es el quince por ciento por encima de este precio.

Señorita Del precio normal, claro.

(el) período period
por encima de above

7 *Lavabo or cuarto de baño?*

Pepe ¿Y lavabo significa cuarto de baño?

Señorita No, lavabo significa solamente, o sea, el lugar ese para, (para, para) lavarse la cara solamente, ¿no?
Luego, está el medio aseo, que ya comprende lavabo y la ducha.
Luego está el baño que lo comprende todo, vamo(s).

Pepe ¿Cuarto de baño?

Señorita Un cuarto de baño completo.

Pepe Bien, bien, muchas gracias.

Señorita De nada.

(el) lugar place
(el) medio aseo shower room
comprende includes
(la) ducha shower
(el) cuarto de baño bathroom
completo complete

6 **la temporada alta son los meses que más turismo hay en la ciudad** the high season is the months when there is most tourism in the city.

quiero decir que entonces hay unos precios establecidos I mean that then there are certain fixed prices. **Querer decir** is an alternative to **significar** **¿qué quiere decir esta señal?** what does this sign mean?

sesenta días al año sixty days a year.

el hotel puede hacer un recargo de un quince por ciento the hotel can make a surcharge of fifteen per cent.

el hotel tiene que especificarlo en recepción the hotel has to specify the fact at the reception desk.

tiene que decírselo al cliente que se está cobrando el quince por ciento por ser la temporada alta (the hotel) has to tell its clients that it's charging 15% extra because of the high season.

7 **lavabo** the literal meaning of this word is wash basin but it is increasingly used as a euphemism for bathroom – hence Pepe's question.

para lavarse la cara solamente to wash your face in only. In Spanish when talking about parts of the body you should translate *your* face, *your* hand as <u>la</u> cara, <u>la</u> mano etc.

vamos well, OK, from **ir** to go.

Key words and phrases

¿qué tal el tiempo?	what's the weather like?
hace frío/calor	it's cold/hot
hace sol/viento	it's sunny/windy
hace buen/mal tiempo	the weather is good/bad
llueve	it's raining
está cubierto	it's overcast
nieva	it's snowing
¿cómo es el clima?	what's the climate like?
el clima es . . .	the climate is . . .
lluvioso	rainy
nubloso	cloudy
seco	dry
caluroso	hot
extremo	extreme
suave	mild
malo	bad
depende de . . .	it depends on . . .
hay niebla	it's foggy
las estaciones del año	the seasons of the year
la primavera	spring
el verano	summer
el otoño	autumn
el invierno	winter

Practice what you have learned

1 You will hear a weather forecast on your tape relating to the map below. Listen to the tape as many times as you need and then answer the following questions by ticking the correct answer. Answers on p. 174

New vocabulary: **(la) tormenta** storm **despejado** clear **nubes alternas** occasional clouds **temperaturas bajas** low temperatures

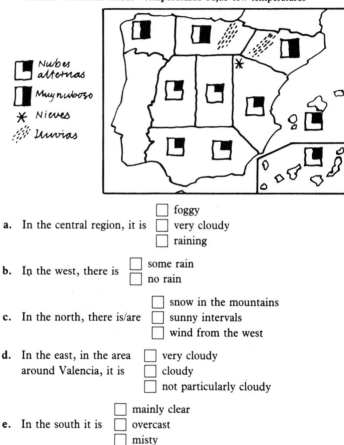

Nubes alternas
Muy nuboso
Nieves
Lluvias

a. In the central region, it is
☐ foggy
☐ very cloudy
☐ raining

b. In the west, there is
☐ some rain
☐ no rain

c. In the north, there is/are
☐ snow in the mountains
☐ sunny intervals
☐ wind from the west

d. In the east, in the area around Valencia, it is
☐ very cloudy
☐ cloudy
☐ not particularly cloudy

e. In the south it is
☐ mainly clear
☐ overcast
☐ misty

2 Can you fill in the missing words in these sentences? A couple of clues: all the words have something to do with the weather and they all begin with **c**! When you have filled in the gaps, check your answers on page 174 of the book.

a. Hace mucho .... en verano en Andalucía.

b. El .... es siempre muy bueno en las islas Baleares.

c. El clima es .... y seco en el sur.

d. Oeste .... en Galicia, con lluvia. (Listen to the weather forecast on your tape again, if you need some extra help on this one.)

3 The clues to this crossword are on tape. Answers on p. 174.

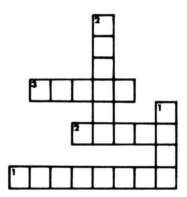

4 Below you have two charts. The first gives you the average temperature on the Costa del Sol and the second gives the water temperature throughout the year. However some of the figures are missing. Listen to the tape and then complete the information below. Answers on p. 174.

Temperatura ambiente de la costa del sol	
	°C
Temperatura media de invierno	....
Temperatura media de primavera	....
Temperatura media de verano	....
Temperatura media de otoño	....
Temperatura media anual	18.7

Temperatura del agua	
enero	15.1
febrero	14.2
marzo	15.2
abril	16.6
mayo	17.4
junio	....
julio	....
agosto	....
septiembre	21.2
octubre	18.3
noviembre	17.8
diciembre	14.4

Grammar

There are three different ways of talking about the weather

1 Using **hacer** to do or make

hace (mucho) calor it's (very) hot
hace buen tiempo it's good weather
hace frío it's cold
hace sol it's sunny
hace mal tiempo the weather is bad

2 Simply saying
el clima es   **bueno** good
               malo bad
               agradable pleasant
               seco dry
               caluroso hot

3 And when you want to be more specific

llueve mucho aquí it rains a lot here
está nevando ahora it's snowing now
no nieva mucho aquí it doesn't snow a lot here
hay niebla it's foggy
está nublado it's cloudy

1 Can you describe these weather conditions? Follow the examples in sections one and three above. For example, (a) would be **hace calor**.

a. ....

b. ....

c. ....

d. ....

....

e. ....

f. ....

g. ....

h. ....

....

Read and understand

```
┌─────────────────────────────────────────────────┐
│        MINISTERIO DE COMERCIO Y TURISMO           │
│          SECRETARIA DE ESTADO DE TURISMO          │
│                    ───                            │
│   Nombre de establecimiento                       │
│   ...... Hotel Brisa del Mar ..........           │
│   Categoría ... 3 estrellas ...............       │
│   Localidad ... Santa Inés ...............        │
│   Provincia ...... Baleares ...............       │
│                                                   │
│   Habitación número ..215...........              │
│   con capacidad para dos personas                 │
│                                                   │
│   Precio de esta habitación:                      │
│                    máximo ... 2,000 ..........    │
│                    mínimo ... 1,600 ..........    │
│                                                   │
│   Servicios sueltos (por persona)                 │
│                    desayuno ..... 150 .......     │
│                    almuerzo ...... 600 .......    │
│                    comida ........ 600 .......    │
│   El precio de la pensión completa es la suma     │
│   de los correspondientes a la habitación y al    │
│   de los servicios sueltos                        │
│   ┌─────────────────────────────────────────┐    │
│   │  Los precios indicados comprenden toda    │   │
│   │           clase de impuestos              │   │
│   └─────────────────────────────────────────┘    │
│   El precio de esta habitación puede aumentarse   │
│   hasta un 15% en las fechas que figuran en el    │
│   cartel en Recepción.                            │
└─────────────────────────────────────────────────┘
```

New vocabulary:
suelto separate
(el) desayuno breakfast
(el) almuerzo lunch
(la) comida dinner

(los) impuestos taxes
aumentarse to increase
(el) cartel notice

Can you answer these questions in Spanish? (If any numbers are required write them out in full.) Answers on p. 174.

1 ¿Cómo se llama el hotel? ....

2 ¿Cuántas estrellas tiene el hotel? ....

3 ¿Dónde está el hotel? ....

4 ¿Cuánto cuesta el almuerzo? ....

5 ¿Los precios comprenden impuestos? ....

Did you know?

Well, you should have picked up something about Spanish weather in this unit. Because Spain is such a large country and so varied in its landscape, the climate also is subject to a great deal of variation from one region to another. So, whatever the season, there is always pleasant weather to be found somewhere *if* you plan your visits carefully.

Spring and autumn are good seasons to go to Spain, but summer in the north and north-west is not usually as hot as you might expect. However, winter on the Mediterranean coast is to be recommended. Madrid and other large inland towns, such as Córdoba and Toledo, get stiflingly hot in summer but are very pleasant in autumn, with agreeable temperatures, clear skies and bright sunshine. So, if you are planning to visit these places at the height of summer, you would do well to be prepared and take the necessary precautions against the sun.

The North coast In Unit 11 Janet mentions that she particularly likes the northern area of Spain. This is also true of the Spanish aristocracy, who usually spend their holidays there. Remember, however, that they are after a cooler climate than the average American holidaymaker. This is a scenically interesting coast because of the background of mountains, called the **Picos de Europa**. Santander is a town worth visiting in this area, and its International University attracts hosts of foreign students in summer. The beaches are marvellous and it is the setting for many regattas and also an international festival of music and dance which is held there in August. Nearby you can visit the famous prehistoric caves of Altamira.

The Ebro basin region, adjoining the Pyrenees, has a very dry, continental climate, being cut off from the sea and almost surrounded by mountains. The Ebro is Spain's second longest river and the grapes for the famous Rioja wines are grown here. Zaragoza, an important city founded by the Romans, is well worth a visit.

In the beautiful **La Concha**, east of Santander, is San Sebastián, a luxurious and cosmopolitan seaside town famous for its film festival, held every September, and also for its bullfights, horse racing, golf championships and exhibitions of modern art.

Córdoba

Your turn to speak

In this conversation you will be describing the weather in England to a Spanish friend. You will need to know **nunca** never.

And finally   As usual, listen to all the dialogues again. You should then test yourself on *Key words and phrases* and on the various expressions you need to describe the weather.

Answers

Practice what you have learned p. 169 Exercise **1** (a) very cloudy (b) some rain (c) snow in the mountains (d) not particularly cloudy (e) mainly clear.

p. 170 Exercise **2** (1) calor (2) clima (3) caluroso (4) cubierto.

p. 170 Exercise **3** Horizontal (1) invierno (2) norte (3) costa. Vertical (1) seco (2) centro.

p. 170 Exercise **4** Temperaturas: (a) invierno 13–14 grados; primavera 20 grados; verano 24 grados; otoño 16 grados. (b) junio, julio, agosto 20 a 22 grados.

Grammar p. 171 (a) hace calor (b) hace frío (c) hace sol (d) hace viento (e) llueve (f) está nevando (g) está nubloso (h) hay niebla

Read and understand p. 172 (1) Hotel Brisa del Mar; (2) tres (3) Santa Inés, Baleares (4) seiscientas pesetas (5) sí.

13 More about yourself

What you will learn

- understanding more about other people's daily routine
- talking about your own
- telling others about your leisure activities
- using reflexive verbs

de paseo

Study guide

	Dialogues 1 – 3: listen straight through without the book
	Dialogues 1 – 3: listen, read and study one by one
	Dialogues 4 – 6: listen straight through without the book
	Dialogues 4 – 6: listen, read and study one by one
	Learn the *Key words and phrases*
	Do the exercises in *Practice what you have learned*
	Study the *Grammar* and do the exercises
	Complete *Read and understand*
	Read *Did you know?*
	Do the tape exercise in *Your turn to speak*
	Listen to all the dialogues
	Test yourself on the *Key phrases* and *Grammar*

Dialogues

1 *Marcos describes his daily routine*

Pepe   Hola.
Marcos Hola.
Pepe   ¿Qué hace usted un día normal?
Marcos Yo me levanto a las seis de la mañana, me visto, me peino, voy al water y arregladito, marcho a la calle, al trabajo.
Pepe   ¿No desayuna?
Marcos Pasadas dos horas, desayuno.
Pepe   ¿En su casa?
Marcos En la calle.
Pepe   ¿En un bar?
Marcos En un bar, efectivamente.
Pepe   Bien ¿y a qué hora comienza a trabajar?
Marcos A las ocho de la mañana.
Pepe   ¿Y a qué hora termina de trabajar?
Marcos Al mediodía, a la una y media del mediodía.

marcho I go
efectivamente precisely

2 *Tere's day*

Rosario ¿Qué hace un día normal?
Tere   Trabajo mucho en la casa y descanso lo que puedo. Me levanto a las siete de la mañana, desayuno, me arreglo, me voy a la oficina, estoy hasta las dos, regreso a casa, almuerzo, hago faenas en la casa, unas veces salgo a la calle de compras o algo, normalmente no salgo, me quedo en casa, leo, veo la tele, así, esas cosas.

(la) oficina office
➤ **regreso** I return
(la) faena job, chore
leo I read
(la) tele TV

1 ◆ **yo me levanto** I get up, **me visto** I get dressed, **me peino** I do my hair. These three verbs **levantarse** to get up, **vestirse** to get dressed and **peinarse** to do one's hair are all termed 'reflexive verbs' (see the *Grammar* section in this unit).

voy al water I go to the lavatory. **Water** pronounced with an initial **v**, is derived from the English 'water closet'. Another commonly used word for lavatory is **(el) retrete**.

arregladito all ready; from the verb **arreglarse** to get oneself ready.

¿no desayuna? don't you have breakfast? **desayunar** to have breakfast, **(el) desayuno** breakfast.

¿a qué hora comienza a trabajar? at what time do you begin work? **comenzar** to begin **comenzar a** to begin to.

¿y a qué hora termina de trabajar? and at what time do you finish work? Note that if you are using **terminar** + another verb you must always use the following construction **terminar** + **de** + verb: **cuando terminas de comer . . .** when you finish eating . . . **¿cuándo termina la película?** when does the film finish?

2 **descanso lo que puedo** I rest (as much) as I can. **Descansar** to rest **(el) descanso** rest.

◆ **me arreglo** I get myself ready.

◆ **almuerzo** I have lunch; **(el) almuerzo** lunch and **almorzar** to have lunch. You've already had **desayunar** and **(el) desayuno** so let's complete the quartet with **cenar** to dine and **(la) cena** dinner and **merendar** to take tea and **(la) merienda** high tea/snack.

salgo a la calle de compras I go out shopping into the street; **salir** is a slightly irregular verb – the full form is given in the *Grammar* section. **Salir de compras** to go out shopping and **comprar** to buy.

esas cosas that sort of thing (lit. those sorts of things).

◆ **me quedo en casa** I stay at home, **quedarse** to remain.

3 *A small boy describes his day*

Pepe   Y tú, ¿a qué hora te levantas?
Javier Yo, a las nueve.
Pepe   ¿Y qué haces después?
Javier Desayuno.
Pepe   ¿Y después?
Javier Pues voy muchas veces al colegio a jugar.
Pepe   ¿Con tus amigos?
Javier Claro.
Pepe   ¿Y a qué hora te acuestas?
Javier Me acuesto (normal . . .) normalmente a las diez.
Pepe   ¿Te gusta mirar la televisión?
Javier Sí.
Pepe   ¿Cuál es tu programa favorito?
Javier Pues 'Cosas'.

después afterwards
jugar to play

4 *Antonio's routine is slightly different, as he is retired*

Antonio Normalmente, pues me levanto a las ocho de la mañana, desayuno
y salgo a las nueve y media o así a darme un paseo por ahí. Y
después al mediodía almorzar y por la tarde mayormente no salgo,
ya me quedo en casa, hasta el día siguiente.
Pepe   ¿No trabaja usted?
Antonio No, porque soy ya jubilado.

por ahí roundabouts
mayormente usually
jubilado retired

3   **y tú ¿a qué hora te levantas?** and you, at what time do you get up? Here is the first example of how the other parts of the reflexive verb work **¿te levantas?** do *you* get up?

¿y a qué hora te acuestas? and at what time do you go to bed? **acostarse** to go to bed. To answer this you would simply reply
♦ **me acuesto a** . . . I go to bed at . . .

¿te gusta mirar la televisión? do you like watching television? In dialogue 2, you had **veo la tele** and this is the more commonly used expression. Strictly speaking **mirar** to look and **ver** to see.

♦ **¿cuál es tu programa favorito?** what is your favourite programme? **programa** is another word like **turista** or **día:** it looks feminine but it is in fact masculine **(el) programa, (el) día, (el) turista. Cosas** is a popular television programme.

4 ♦ **salgo . . . a darme un paseo por ahí** I go out for a walk in the neighbourhood. **Me** has been tagged on to the end of **dar** to give because it's used in the infinitive. More about this in *Grammar.*
♦ **dar un paseo** to go for a walk; **doy un paseo** I go for a walk.

después al mediodía almorzar then at midday I have lunch. **Almorzar** is being used here as a noun, hence its infinitive form.

♦ **hasta el día siguiente** until the next day.

5 *Now Pilar turns the tables on Pepe and ask him what he does*

Pilar   ¿A qué hora se levanta?
Pepe   Normalmente a las siete de la mañana.
Pilar   ¿Y a qué hora se acuesta normalmente?
Pepe   A las once y media o las doce de la noche.
Pilar   ¿Duerme usted la siesta?
Pepe   Normalmente no, en verano sí, pero en invierno nunca.

6 *A family plans an outing*

Pablo   ¿Qué vamos a hacer hoy?
Padre   No sé. Hoy vamos a visitar el pueblo.
Pablo   No, yo quiero ir a otro sitio.
Padre   Primero vamos a visitar el pueblo.
Pablo   Quiero ir al zoológico.
Javier   No, yo quiero ir al cine.
Juan   No, yo quiero quedarme aquí a ver la tele.
Alejandro   No, yo voy a montarme en bicicleta.
Jaime   No, no, yo quiero ir a bailar con mis amigos.
Padre   Pues estos niños, que se vayan a algún sitio porque yo quiero ver
            tranquilo el partido que van a televisar.

(el) zoológico zoo
(el) cine cinema
bailar to dance
tranquilo in peace
(el) partido match
televisar to televize

5 ¿a qué hora se levanta? at what time do you get up?

¿a qué hora se acuesta? at what time do you go to bed? Here are two examples **se levanta** and **se acuesta** of the reflexive form for yourself, himself, herself.

¿duerme usted la siesta? do you take a siesta? **duerme** is from **dormir** to sleep; **echar una siesta** to have a siesta.

6 ♦ ¿qué vamos a hacer hoy? what are we going to do today? Note that **ir** to go but **ir a** to be about to.
vamos a visitar we are going to visit.
voy a hacerlo I'm going to do it.

More examples of this use of **ir a** in the next unit.

no, yo voy a montarme en bicicleta no, I'm going to ride my bicycle. Here's another example of **me** being tagged on to an infinitive; and see the line above **quiero quedarme** I want to stay.

pues, estos niños que se vayan a algún sitio well, let these children all go off somewhere.

Key words and phrases

¿qué hace usted un día normal?	what do you do on a typical day?
me levanto	I get up
me visto	I get dressed
me peino	I do my hair
me arreglo	I get ready
me acuesto	I go to bed
doy un paseo	I go for a walk
salgo (de compras)	I go out (shopping)
¿qué vamos a hacer?	what are we going to do?
voy a echar una siesta	I'm going to have a siesta
me quedo en casa	I stay at home
regreso a la oficina	I return to the office
quiero ver (la tele)	I want to watch (TV)
quiero ir (al cine)	I want to go (to the cinema)
el día siguiente	the next day
¿cuál es tu programa favorito?	which is your favourite programme?
(el) desayuno	breakfast
(el) almuerzo	lunch
(la) merienda	snack
(la) cena	dinner
desayunar/almorzar/merendar/ cenar	to breakfast/to lunch/to take tea/to dine

Practice what you have learned

1 Imagine you are the woman whose morning routine is illustrated below. Answer the questions you will hear on the tape about what you will be doing tomorrow morning. Answer out loud and also write it in the space provided. Answers on p. 188.

a. .... b. .... c. .... d. ....

....

e. .... f. .... g. ....

....

2 The left hand column below gives the times at which Miguel performs various activities and the right hand column lists the activities. Unfortunately, the two do not correspond: can you try matching them up? Write in the correct number in the space provided and *then* listen to the tape where you will hear Miguel describing his daily routine.

A las seis y media ....   **1** me visto

A las siete menos cuarto ....   **2** comienzo a desayunar

      3 trabajo en la oficina

A las siete y cinco ....   **4** regreso a casa

A las siete y media ....   **5** ceno

Desde las ocho de la mañana a las   **6** me levanto
dos de la tarde ....

A las dos de la tarde ....   **7** salgo a la oficina

A las tres ....   **8** me acuesto

Desde las tres hasta las nueve   **9** salgo a almorzar

....

A las nueve ....   **10** hago faenas, salgo a dar

A las once de la noche ....   un paseo, leo

UNIT 13   183

3 Beatriz was interviewed about her daily routine. Her replies are given in the box below. Can you write them in the correct order? When you have completed the dialogue, check your answers against those on p. 188.

Miguel   Beatriz, quiero saber lo que haces un día normal.

Beatriz   ....

Miguel   Pues sí.

Beatriz   ....

Miguel   ¿Y después del desayuno?

Beatriz   ....

          ....

Miguel   ¿Y qué haces a la una y media?

Beatriz   ....

          ....

Miguel   ¿Y después del almuerzo?

Beatriz   ....

          ....

Miguel   ¿Y después de eso regresas a casa?

Beatriz   ....

          ....

Miguel   Bien – ¿y a qué hora te acuestas?

Beatriz   ....

          ....

Beatriz's replies

A la una de la noche aproximadamente.
¿Lo que hago un día normal?
Pues almuerzo en un restaurante cerca del colegio
Uy, muchas cosas, me levanto a las seis y desayuno.
Vuelvo al trabajo y estoy allí hasta las cinco o las cinco y media
Después del desayuno, voy al trabajo y estoy allí hasta la una y media.
Normalmente, sí. Regreso a casa y leo, veo la tele, algunas veces me arreglo y salgo a dar un paseo.

Grammar

Reflexive verbs

In English if you say 'I'm getting up' you mean you are going to get *yourself* up; if you say you are going to wash, it is understood that you will be washing yourself. In Spanish you have to specify that you yourself will be doing it by using a 'reflexive' verb. This is just the grammatical term used when you are doing something to or for yourself, e.g. **levantarse**/ to get (oneself) up; **vestirse**/ to get (oneself) dressed. Here is the pattern followed by all reflexive verbs in the present tense:

<u>me</u> **levanto**   <u>nos</u> **levantamos**
<u>te</u> **levantas**   <u>os</u> **levantáis**
<u>se</u> **levanta**   <u>se</u> **levantan**

Note 1   You must use *both* parts of the verb when using the verb reflexively: you cannot use the **levantamos** without the **nos**.

2   The pronouns **me, te, se, nos, os, se** must always come in front of the verb *unless* the verb is in the infinitive in which case they should be tagged on the end of the infinitive.

voy a levantarme a las siete de la mañana
I'm going to get up at seven o'clock in the morning

1   Match the pronouns to the verbs supplied. Answers on p. 188.

a. .... van.

b. .... arreglamos.

c. .... quedas.

d. .... levanto.

e. .... peináis.

f. .... acuesta.

ellos se   se   *me*

os

nos   *te*

Salir   to go, to leave

salgo   **salimos**
sales   **salís**
sale   **salen**

2   Fill in the blanks with the correct form of the verb **salir**. Answers on p. 188.

a.   yo .... de compras.

b.   mi padre .... a la calle a trabajar a las seis.

c.   nosotros .... de paseo antes de la cena.

d.   ellas .... de la oficina a las dos de la tarde.

e.   ¿ por qué no .... vosotros a jugar?

Read and understand

Here is an extract from an interview with Marisol, the well-known Spanish pop star.

> ## Marisol
>
> Bien, cuando no trabajo, me levanto muy tarde – a eso de las diez o las once de la mañana porque normalmente me levanto muy temprano para ir a trabajar. Pero si no trabajo, me levanto tarde y desayuno primero, antes de vestirme. Cuando termino el desayuno, me arreglo, me peino, me visto y salgo a la calle de compras, para mirar las tiendas o tomo algo en un bar con mis amigas. A las dos, o así voy a mi restaurante favorito – un restaurante típico cerca del piso en que vivo y almuerzo – sola o con amigas – luego regreso a casa y descanso, duermo la siesta en verano, leo o veo la tele en el invierno. A eso de las siete, o siete y media, me arreglo otra vez y salgo de paseo, vamos a una cafetería y tomamos café o vino. Luego a casa otra vez a cenar y después, me acuesto o algunas veces voy al cine con mi novio o voy a bailar . . . así, esas cosas.
> Bien, Marisol, gracias.

New vocabulary:
temprano early
tomo algo I have a drink of something (**tomar** to take)

Delete the statements which are incorrect. Answers on p. 188.

1 Marisol gets up early / late when she's not working

2 In the evening after dinner she plays cards / goes dancing / watches television

3 The restaurant she eats at is a fast food restaurant / is a cafeteria / serves traditional Spanish meals

4 She never has a siesta / always has a siesta / has one in summer

5 She has got a boyfriend / has not got a boyfriend

Did you know?

Breakfast customs

In dialogue 1 of this unit, Marcos tells Pepe that he usually breakfasts in a bar two hours after having started work. This is quite a common practice, particularly among manual workers. A breakfast taken in a bar will often consist of a glass of cognac or wine. Most Spanish people favour a light breakfast of coffee or hot chocolate with rolls or **tostadas** – large pieces of cold toast spread with margarine. Sometimes they will send out for **churros**: these taste rather like doughnuts but are long and thin in shape. There are **churros** stands on almost every corner in Spain and they are open until late at night. **Chocolate con churros** is often featured on menus: the chocolate will be thick enough to make your spoon stand up and the **churros** will be served hot with sugar.

El paseo

This is a uniquely Spanish custom that takes place in Spanish towns and villages before dinner – i.e. from eight o'clock onwards. Families and friends dress up and then procede to walk around the town. Most places have particular 'spots' for walking e.g. the **Herradura** in Santiago: people are simply out to pass the time, gossip etc.

La siesta

This is a custom which is being observed less and less these days. The habit has always been more widespread in the south but in northern Spain it has now almost vanished. However, it's still very much in use in southern Spain during the summer so you would be best advised not to try to get anywhere between 3 and 5 p.m. Andalusians will often work right through without a break until 2 or 3 p.m. and then have their lunch followed by a siesta. Refreshed, they will begin life anew **de paseo**, visiting bars etc. This applies equally to children, so don't be surprised to find young children around with their parents until quite late at night.

Your turn to speak

In this dialogue you will be asked to describe your daily routine. You will be practicing many of the reflexive verbs you have met in this unit and as you will be asked what you do at a specific time of day, it may be worth your while reviewing Unit 6 on *Time*.

As a quick check on how much you can remember, try translating the following (answers at the foot of the page): a quarter past eleven, half-past six, twenty to nine, a quarter to five, it's four o'clock.

And finally Listen to all the dialogues again and test yourself on the *Key words and phrases*. To check that you understand reflexive verbs, try writing out **arreglarse** (to get oneself ready) in the present tense. (Answers at foot of page.)

Answers

Practice what you have learned p.183 Exercise 1 (a) me levanto a las siete de la mañana (b) me lavo a las siete y cuarto (c) me peino a las siete y veinticinco (d) me arreglo/me visto a las siete y media (e) desayuno a las ocho menos cuarto (f) salgo de la casa a las ocho (g) llego a la oficina a las ocho y media.

p. 184 Exercise 3 Beatriz, quiero saber lo que haces un día normal./ ¿Lo que hago un día normal?/ Pues sí./ Uy, muchas cosas, me levanto a las seis y desayuno./ ¿Y después del desayuno?/ Después del desayuno, voy al trabajo y estoy allí hasta la una y media./ ¿Y qué haces a la una y media?/ Pues almuerzo en un restaurante cerca del colegio./ ¿Y después del almuerzo?/ Vuelvo al trabajo y estoy allí hasta las cinco o las cinco y media./ ¿Y después de eso, regresas a casa?/ Normalmente, sí. Regreso a casa y leo, veo la tele, algunas veces me arreglo y salgo a dar un paseo./ Bien – ¿y a qué hora te acuestas?/ A la una de la noche aproximadamente.

Grammar p. 185 Exercise 1 (a) ellos se van (b) nos arreglamos (c) te quedas (d) me levanto (e) os peináis (f) se acuesta

p. 185 Exercise 2 (a) salgo (b) sale (c) salimos (d) salen (e) salís.

Read and understand p. 186 (1) Marisol gets up late. (2) She goes dancing. (3) She eats in a restaurant that serves traditional meals. (4) She has a siesta in the summer. (5) She has got a boyfriend.

Your turn to speak p. 188 time: las once y cuarto, las seis y media, las nueve menos veinte, las cinco menos cuarto, son las cuatro.

p. 188 Arreglarse: me arreglo, te arreglas, se arregla, nos arreglamos, os arregláis, se arreglan.

14 Stating your intentions

What you will learn

- asking questions about the future
- talking about the future
- asking for directions
- something about Spanish theatres and cinemas

Before you begin

You've already learnt one way of talking about the future **ir a** + infinitive = to be going to + infinitive: **voy a trabajar mañana** I'm going to work tomorrow. In Spanish, as in English, you can also talk about the future by using the future tense of the verb e.g. **trabajaré mañana** I will work tomorrow.

However, in Spanish if you want to get over the idea that you *must* do something, you can use **tengo que ... I** have to ... **tengo que trabajar mañana** I have to work tomorrow.

Study hint   Remember the motto 'little and often'. It is more valuable to spend a few minutes every day thinking in Spanish than to immerse yourself in the language once every few weeks. When you have finished this unit, why not try each evening for a week to make up a few sentences about your day's activities and describe your plans for tomorrow's?

Study guide

	Dialogues 1 – 4: listen, straight through without the book
	Dialogues 1 – 4: listen, read and study one by one
	Dialogues 5 – 7: listen straight through without the book
	Dialogues 5 – 7: listen, read and study one by one
	Study the *Key words and phrases*
	Do the exercises in *Practice what you have learned*
	Study the *Grammar* and do the exercise
	Complete *Read and understand*
	Read *Did you know?*
	Do the tape exercise in *Your turn to speak*
	Listen to all the dialogues again

Dialogues

1 *This evening's plans*

Alvaro	¿Qué vamos a hacer hoy?
Neni	No sé ¿qué te apetece?
Alvaro	¿Vamos a la discoteca?
Neni	Echan una buena obra de teatro. ¿Te parece que vayamos al teatro?
Alvaro	Bien y ¿adónde ir después del teatro?
Neni	Podemos ir a un restaurante a cenar.
Alvaro	Perfectamente. Creo que me gustará mucho.

(la) discoteca discotheque
perfectamente good idea

2 *Making plans for Saturday*

Sandra	Mañana es sábado. ¿Qué hará usted?
María de los Angeles	Pues lo siguiente: me levantaré a las ocho de la mañana, tomaré un baño como de costumbre. Desayunaré ligeramente y después saldré de compras. Por la tarde, tengo dos nietas muy bonitas y las sacaré de paseo.

lo siguiente the following
como de costumbre as usual
(la) nieta grand-daughter

1 ♦ **¿qué vamos a hacer hoy?** what are we going to do today? You might reply
♦ **vamos a . . .** we're going to . . . or
♦ **voy a . . .** I'm going to. Don't forget to put the verb that follows into the
infinitive! **voy a trabajar** I'm going to work.

♦ **¿qué te apetece?** what do you feel like doing? If talking to someone you
don't know well, simply substitue **le** for **te ¿qué le apetece?** This
expression can also be used to ask someone what they fancy having in a
restaurant or bar **¿le apetece pescado?** do you fancy the fish?

echan una buena obra de teatro there's a good play on. **Una obra de
teatro** is a play and **echar** you have already met in an earlier unit **echar
una siesta** to have a siesta. **Echar** literally means 'to throw' but you will
find it used in many phrases such as **echarse a reír** to start laughing/to
burst out laughing; **echar a correr** to start running/to break into a run.

¿te parece que vayamos al teatro? what about going to the theatre? You
are far more likely to be asked **¿qué le parece . . .?** what do you think
of . . .?

♦ **podemos ir a un restaurante** we could go to a restaurant. If you are asked
your opinion **¿qué le parece ir a la piscina?** what do you think about
going to the swimming pool?, you can always suggest an alternative
¿podemos ir al partido de fútbol? could we go to the soccer match?

♦ **creo que me gustará mucho** I think I'd like that very much. Note that in
the third person the future tense is formed by adding an –á to the infinitive
form of the verb **¿comerá?** will you eat?

2 **¿qué hará usted?** what will you do? Sandra could also have asked **¿qué
va a hacer usted?** what are you going to do?

♦ **tomaré un baño** I'll have a bath; **tomar un baño** to have a bath; **tomar
una ducha** to have a shower. Note that the future tense is formed by
putting an **-é** on the infinitive form of the verb **tomaré** I will have . . .
There are two further examples of this in **me levantaré** I will get up, and
desayunaré I will breakfast.

saldré de compras I'll go shopping. This is the future tense of **salir**, one
of the few verbs which has an irregular future (See *Grammar* p. 199.)

las sacaré de paseo I will take them out for a walk. **Sacar de paseo** to
take for a walk, more commonly used with reference to pets!

3 *Juan talks about his plans*

Juan   Tengo que ir al ayuntamiento porque tengo que ir a retirar unos documentos que me tienen que entregar.

Sandra   Muy bien, y ¿qué hará después usted?

Juan   Después, bueno, pasaré a tomar un refrigerio con unos amigos y nos pondremos de acuerdo para ir a almorzar juntos.

Sandra   Muy bien.

retirar to take out, collect
(el) documento document
entregar to give, hand over
juntos together

4 *At the hairdresser's*

José   ¿Qué tal señora? ¿Cómo se lo voy a cortar a usted?

José   Se lo voy a cortar de arriba, porque está muy largo y tiene mucho peso, entonces se le va a caer mucho, ¿eh? Se va a secar con secadora de mano hoy, ¿no?

María   Sí, sí.

arriba up
largo long
(el) peso weight
caer to fall
secar to dry

5 *Pepe asks for directions to Chipiona*

Pepe   Por favor, ¿para ir a Chipiona, a la playa de Chipiona?

Neni   Pues puede coger dos camino(s). Uno por la autopista hacia Cádiz y otro por la carretera nacional cuatro.

Pepe   ¿Y hay que pagar en la autopista?

Neni   Sí, tiene que pagar peaje.

Pepe   ¿Y para ir por la carretera nacional, es directo hasta Chipiona?

Neni   No, en Jerez de la Frontera se desviará hacia la derecha por la carretera 440 a Sanlúcar de Barrameda. En Sanlúcar, dejará esa carretera y cogerá hacia la izquierda por la 441.

(la) playa beach
(el) camino way, road
(el) peaje toll
se desviará you turn off
dejará you will leave
cogerá you will take

3   Juan is from Argentina and he speaks with a slightly different accent: in particular listen to the way in which he pronounces *z*.

♦ **tengo que ir al ayuntamiento** I have to go to the town hall. Juan uses **tengo que** instead of **voy a**, because he has *got* to go.

pasaré a tomar un refrigerio I'll drop in to have a cool drink. **Refrigerio** can also mean a 'snack' but as Juan goes on to talk about having lunch, you can safely assume that here he must be talking about a drink.

nos pondremos de acuerdo we'll decide to . . . The infinitive form of 'to agree' is **ponerse de acuerdo. Poner** is an irregular verb and introduces **d** in the future tense. You've already met another verb which follows this pattern **salir** to go **saldré** I will go; **poner** to put and **pondré** I will put. (See *Grammar* p. 199.)

4   **¿cómo se le voy a cortar a usted?** how am I going to cut your hair?

5 ♦ **¿y hay que pagar en la autopista?** and do you have to pay on the motorway? **hay que** = **tiene que** one must, but it never changes: **hay que ir todo seguido** you've got to go straight on and **¿hay que hacerlo?** must one do it?

6 *And for directions to Utrera*

Pepe Por favor, ¿para ir a Utrera?
Alvaro Toma la autopista para Cádiz hasta la altura de Dos Hermanas. Lo atraviesa. Encontrará un cruce con la carretera 432, en cuyo cruce girará a izquierda y seguirá hacia Utrera.
Pepe ¿Qué distancia aproximadamente hay desde aquí hasta Utrera, por favor?
Alvaro Unos treinta kilómetros.
Pepe Gracias.

lo atraviesa you cross it
encontrará you will find
(el) cruce junction
girará you will turn

6 **hasta la altura de Dos Hermanas** till you get to Dos Hermanas; **altura** (lit.) height. **Dos Hermanas** is the name of a place but it also translates as Two Sisters.

en cuyo cruce at this crossroads.

♦ **¿qué distancia hay desde aquí hasta Utrera?** how far is it from here to Utrera?

7 *Alejandro tells Pepe about his plans for the next day*

Pepe ¿Qué vas a hacer mañana?
Alejandro Yo, me levantaré y despué(s) me iré un momentito al cole a jugar, vendré y veré la tele un poco. Pue(s), comeré y pue(s) iré al cine a verlo y despué(s). . .
Pepe ¿Qué (qué) película irás a ver?
Alejandro El Libro de la Selva . . .

veré I'll watch
(la) película film

7 **me iré un momentito al cole a jugar** I'll go to school for a while to play. Alejandro says **momentito** (**momento** + diminutive **ito**) because he doesn't really intend to stay very long; and **cole** is slang for **(el) colegio** school.

vendré I'll come back.

pues, iré al cine a verlo then, I'll go to the cinema to see it. Alejandro actually says **irá** but as you can see it doesn't stop Pepe understanding him. Pepe then asks him what film he's going to see and his nephew replies **El Libro de la Selva** *The Jungle Book.*

Key words and phrases

¿qué vamos a hacer?	what are we going to do?
vamos a (dar un paseo)	we are going to (go for a walk)
voy a (salir de compras)	I'm going to (go shopping)
tengo que (ir allí)	I must (go there)
hay que (verlo)	you must (see it)
¿qué (te, le) apetece?	what do you feel like?
podemos ir a (una discoteca)	we could go to (a discothèque)
me gustará mucho	I'd like that very much

And the future

me levantaré	I will get up
tomaré un baño	I will have a bath
me arreglaré	I will get ready
cogeré un autobús	I will catch a bus

And some more directions

¿qué distancia hay desde aquí hasta (Utrera)?	how far is it from here to (Utrera)?
¿es directo hasta (Marchena)?	is it direct to (Marchena)?

Practice what you have learned

1 Listen to the news bulletin on your tape and then tick the statements you believe to be correct. Answers on p. 202.

New vocabulary:
participará he will take part
(el) acto function
habrá there will be
(las) elecciones elections

1 There will be elections in Sevilla and Córdoba on the
- [ ] **a.** 27th
- [ ] **b.** 22nd
- [ ] **c.** 24th

2 The Spanish President will take part in
- [ ] **a.** three
- [ ] **b.** four functions
- [ ] **c.** two

3 On the 6th of December don Juan Carlos and doña Sofia, the King and Queen of Spain will attend
- [ ] **a.** the opera in Milan
- [ ] **b.** a cinema festival in Rome
- [ ] **c.** a concert in Turin

4 On the 7th they will go to
- [ ] **a.** the first night of a new film
- [ ] **b.** a play directed by Franco Martinelli
- [ ] **c.** an official banquet

5 What is Tomás Fernández' job?
- [ ] **a.** Secretary to the Town Hall
- [ ] **b.** President of the local branch of UCD
- [ ] **c.** Director of Plástico Valenciano S.A.

2 Now listen to the dialogue on the tape which takes place in a travel agency. You'll hear the girl telling Antonio about a holiday especially organized for retired people **los jubilados**. Listen to it a couple of times, if necessary taking notes and then try filling in the omitted words in the promotional leaflet below. Answers on p. 202.

New vocabulary:
(la) **oferta** offer
(el) **barco** boat
a bordo on board
(el) **puerto** port
(la) **actividad** activity

SENSACIONAL
....
PARA
....
.... **DE GANDIA**

Día 1 PALMA – VALENCIA
Salida en barco a las 23′00 h.
Noche ....

Día 2 VALENCIA – GANDIA
Llegada a Valencia a las ....
salida en autocar hacia Gandía. Almuerzo, cena.

Día 7 GANDIA – VALENCIA – PALMA
Desayuno y almuerzo en el hotel. Por la tarde a última
hora después de la cena traslado al
.... de Valencia. Salida en
.... a las 23′00 h. Noche a bordo.

POR PERSONA 8.050 – PTAS
Mínimo 40 participantes
Este precio .... billetes de barco ida y
vuelta
Estancia en el Hotel Las Anclas en Gandía
Categoría .... estrellas
Pensión completa. Incluído .... en las
comidas.

HOTEL LAS ANCLAS
Características: salón social, piscina, parque infantil,
todas las .... con baño
.... calefacción.

---

3 Listen to the conversation on tape between Montse and her hairdresser Jesus. Listed below are some of the services and treatments on offer at *Vicens*. Tick or put a cross in the box according to whether or not Montse wanted that particular service or treatment. If some of the treatments are not mentioned on tape, leave the boxes blank. Answers on p. 202.

New vocabulary:

marcar to set
(la) manicura manicure
(el) estilo style
reflejos colorantes highlights
revitalizante conditioning
moldeadora soft perm

según calidad de
  esmalte according to the quality
  of nail polish
(el) champú shampoo
(el) oro gold
(la) plata silver

Peluquería
VICENS

	Servicios	*Tarifas*
1 ☐	*Lavar y marcar*	*300 ptas*
2 ☐	*Cortar*	*450*
3 ☐	*Lavar/broshing (secadora de mano)*	*350*
4 ☐	*Crema revitalizante*	*300*
5 ☐	*Loción para marcar*	*200*
6 ☐	*Reflejos colorantes*	*450*
7 ☐	*Manicura (según calidad de esmalte)*	*200/450*
8 ☐	*Moldeadora*	*1500*
9 ☐	*Permanente en frío*	*1400*
10 ☐	*Champú 'oro y plata'*	*300*

Grammar

Talking about the future

You will have noted during the course of the dialogues that there are three ways of doing this in Spanish.

1 If you *have* to do something, use **tengo que** . . .

tengo que ir a retirar unos documentos	I've got to go and collect some documents
usted tiene que venir a Inglaterra	you must come to England

2 If you just *want* to do something then use **ir a** . . .

voy a (ir al cine)	I'm going to (go to the cinema)
¿usted va a (venir conmigo)?	are you going to (come with me)?

3 If you want to be a little more formal, use the future tense

me levantaré más tarde	I will get up later

Forming the future tense

Take the infinitive form of the verb (**-ar**, **-er**, **-ir**) and then add the following endings. e.g. **comprar** to buy

(yo) **-é**	**compraré**	(nosotros) **-emos**	**compraremos**
(tu) **-ás**	**comprarás**	(vosotros) **-éis**	**compraréis**
(el, ella, vd.) **-á**	**comprará**	(ellos/ellas/vds.) **-an**	**comprarán**

The endings remain the same if it is an **-er** or **-ir** verb: **comer** to eat, **comeré** I will eat; **escribir** to write, **escribiré** I will write.

Some verbs, examples of which you have already come across in this unit, do not conform exactly to this pattern although they do keep the same endings. The stems (or the first parts) of these verbs change, usually with the introduction of a **d**. Here are some examples:

poner	**pondré**	I will put
tener que	**tendrás que**	you will have to
venir	**vendrá**	he will come
salir	**saldremos**	we will go out
poder	**podréis**	you will be able
hacer	**harán**	they will do

1 Fill in the blanks with the Spanish translation of the phrases. Answers p. 202

1 (I've got to) .... salir de compras mañana.

2 (I'm going to watch) .... el partido de fútbol.

3 (I'm going to go to) .... al cine mañana en Ronda.

4 ¿Cuándo .... (shall I pay)?

5 (I'll get up) ....:.... muy temprano mañana.

Read and understand

Here is an extract from a letter that Fina writes to her parents. She is on holiday in Ibiza and writes to describe what she, her husband and children will be doing tomorrow.

Y mañana – mañana vamos a visitar la capital de la isla, que también se llama Ibiza. Parece que es una ciudad muy bonita construída en una montaña cerca del mar. Iremos a estos barrios famosos, muy blancos, en donde se puede ver el mar abajo... Seguro que es precioso ¿verdad? Tendremos que ir también a visitar el ayuntamiento y la catedral que están en el barrio de Dalt Vila. Parece que tiene murallas del siglo <u>XVI</u> que le gustarán mucho a Juan. Pero los niños no estarán contentos si no vamos a la playa, así que después de almorzar en la ciudad, iremos a la playa más cerca del hotel y jugarán allí con otros niños también del hotel. Pero antes tendré que ir de compras.

Muchos besos y abrazos de tu hija,
Fina

New vocabulary:
construída built
(el) barrio district, quarter
seguro surely
precioso lovely
(la) muralla rampart
(el) siglo century
(el) beso kiss
(el) abrazo embrace

How many examples of the future can you find in this letter? Underline them in the passage and then check them against the answers on p. 204.

Did you know?

The theatre

Most Spanish theatres are concentrated in the larger cities as these are the only places capable of supporting theatre companies. Madrid has some thirty theatres and the works of many modern playwrights can be seen there. When these move to Barcelona which has the second largest concentration of theatres, many of the plays are performed in Catalan. So if you're planning a visit to the theatre in Barcelona, check beforehand what language the play will be in!

There are usually two shows an evening: one at about 7 p.m., the other at about 10:30 – 11 p.m. If you want a good seat ask for the **butacas** (stalls) or even a **palco** (box). If you're looking for a cheap night's entertainment try the **anfiteatro** (the balcony). Consult the local newspaper to find out what's on and at what time the performance starts; look under the heading **cartelera**. You will be shown to your seat by an **acomodadora** (usherette) to whom you should give a tip of a couple of pesetas. (This also applies to cinema usherettes.)

If you think your command of Spanish is not sufficient enough to understand a play, why not try a **zarzuela** (a light operetta)? It's Spain's answer to Gilbert and Sullivan and you would never see a performance outside the country.

Cinemas

Cinemas in Spain continue to be very popular. Most films are imported from the United States, France or Italy and they are usually dubbed. As at the theatre, there are usually two programmes a day, one at 7 p.m. and one at 10 p.m. Should you visit a cinema in Spain, be prepared for some 'audience participation'. Spanish people like action films and boo and hiss the 'baddie' and hero accordingly. They also eat a lot of popcorn and sunflower seeds **pipas**. And finally, smoking is forbidden in both cinema and theatres.

Your turn to speak

In this exercise you will be telling Mari about your plans for tomorrow. You will be practicing **voy a** . . . and as you will have to specify at what time you will be doing certain things, we suggest that you review Unit 6 on time unless you are sure you now know it!

And finally Listen to all the dialogues again and test yourself on the *Key words and phrases*. Now that you know how to express yourself in the future, why not try describing *out loud* what you will do when you travel to Spain.

Answers

Practice what you have learned p. 196 Exercise **1** (**1**) (a) (**2**) (c) (**3**) (b) (**4**) (b) (**5**) (a))

p. 197 Exercise **2**: the missing words were in chronological order: oferta/ jubilados/playa/a bordo/a las ocho/puerto/barco/incluye/tres/vino/ habitaciones/completa

p. 198 Exercise **3** You should have ticked (2) (3) (10); crossed (1) (7) and left the remaining numbers blank.

Grammar p. 199 Exercise **1** (**1**) tengo que (**2**) voy a ver (**3**) voy a ir (**4**) pagaré (**5**) me levantaré

Read and understand p. 200 There were eight futures; vamos a visitar/ iremos/tendremos que ir/nos gustarán mucho/estarán/iremos/jugarán/ tendré que ir

15 Talking about the past

What you will learn

- describing past holidays
- describing past leisure activities
- some more airport vocabulary
- something about Cuenca and the area around Valencia

Before you begin

This is the last unit of the course. You should find the language you have learnt here of value if you go to a Spanish-speaking country. You've learnt enough to get by and to carry on straightforward conversations. Try to keep practising Spanish when you have finished the course. Even if you don't have a chance to practise speaking regularly with Spanish speakers, try not to let your language skills get rusty. Take every opportunity to read or speak Spanish, even if only for a few minutes at a time.

Study guide

	Dialogues 1 – 3: listen straight through without the book
	Dialogues 1 – 3: listen, read and study one by one
	Dialogues 4 – 7: listen straight through without the book
	Dialogues 4 – 7: listen, read and study one by one
	Learn the *Key words and phrases*
	Do the exercises in *Practice what you have learned*
	Study *Grammar* and do the exercise
	Complete *Read and understand*
	Read *Did you know?*
	Do *Your turn to speak*
	Listen to the dialogues again
	Test yourself on the *Key words* and the verbs from *Grammar*
	Do the revision/review exercises on p. 220

Dialogues

1 *A trip to England*

Pepe ¿Conoce usted Inglaterra?
Tere Sí, estuve en Inglaterra hace dos años.
Pepe ¿Le gustó a usted Inglaterra?
Tere Sí, sí, me gustó mucho.
Pepe ¿Qué ciudades le gustaron más?
Tere Me gustaron mucho la ciudad de Bath y Bristol.
Pepe ¿Qué es lo que le gustó menos de Inglaterra?
Tere Lo que me gustó meno(s) es que los inglese(s) hablan inglés en vez de hablar español. ¡Qué difícil e(s) el inglé(s)!

en vez de instead of

2 *Neni recounts her day*

Neni Primero fui al colegio a llevar a lo(s) niño(s). Luego, quise buscar la tienda que me habían dicho de antigüedades. Me perdí. Después, al cabo de mucho tiempo de andar, conseguí llegar. Compré aquel quinqué que tanto nos gustaba. Y luego fui de tienda(s) a ver el traje para la pequeña.

(las) antigüedades antiques
al cabo de at the end of, after
andar to walk
conseguí I managed
(el) traje outfit

1 ♦ **estuve en Inglaterra hace dos años** I was in England two years ago. The first example of a past tense is unfortunately an irregular one: **estuve** I was (from **estar**). The expression **hace dos años** two years ago will be easy to memorize as the form never changes, you merely substitute the correct number of years: **hace cuatro años estuve en Londres de vacaciones** four years ago I was on holiday in London; **estuve allí hace treinta años** I was there thirty years ago.

♦ **¿le gustó a usted Inglaterra?** did you like England?

♦ **me gustó mucho** I liked it a lot.

¿qué ciudades le gustaron más? which cities did you like most? Because cities is plural (**ciudades**) **gustaron** must also be plural. An easy way to remember this is to translate the phrase quickly in your head as 'what cities pleased you most?'

la ciudad de Bath y Bristol either a slip of the tongue by Tere – she should, of course, have said **las ciudades de Bath y Bristol** – or she believes Bath and Bristol to be one and the same thing!

2 ♦ **fui al colegio a llevar a los niños** I took the children to school. **Fui** (from **ir**) I went/I was; **fui ayer**, I went yesterday.

quise buscar la tienda que me habían dicho I wanted to find the shop they'd told me about. **quise** = I wanted, another irregular past but as you will hear words like **quise, estuve, fui** used frequently, they will soon come naturally to you.

♦ **me perdí** I got lost. This is a regular past tense; **-ir** and **-er** verbs in the first person in the past tense end in **í**: **viví** (**vivir**) I lived; **escribí** (**escribir**) I wrote; **salí** (**salir**) I went out, **comí** (**comer**) I ate; **bebí** (**beber**) I drank; **ví** (**ver**) I saw.

♦ **compré aquel quinqué** I bought that lamp. Here is an example of an **-ar** verb in the past tense: **comprar** (to buy) becomes **compré** = I bought; **hablar** (to speak) becomes **hablé** = I spoke; **llevar** (to take) **llevé** = I took. As you will see from these examples, the past is easy to form in the first person singular: simply substitute **é** for the **-ar** ending.

que tanto nos gustaba that we liked so much.

fui de tiendas I went shopping. An alternative to **salir de compras** which you have already learnt; **fui de tiendas/salí de compras con mi amiga** = I went shopping with my friend.

3 *A breakdown*

Luisa	¿Se le averió el coche?
Antonio	Sí, se nos averió. Por eso llegamos tarde.
Luisa	¿Fue una avería importante?
Antonio	No, no fue nada grave.
Luisa	¿Estuvo muchos días el coche en el garaje?
Antonio	Dos días.
Luisa	¿Fue esta la primera vez?
Antonio	No. Tuvimos otra el domingo y fue peor porque no pudimos encontrar un garaje abierto.
Luisa	Vaya, lo siento, hombre.

4 *A day on the beach*

Juan   El domingo pasado, bueno, como tenía libre, éste . . . también me levanté muy temprano, y como me atrae mucho la vida al aire libre, estuve en la playa con unos amigos, pasamos la mañana allí, estuvimos nadando un poco y entreteniéndonos en la arena, jugando un poco al fútbol.

(la) **arena** the sand
pasamos we spent

3 ¿se le averió el coche? did your car break down? If referring to él or ella or usted in the past tense the ending is ó or ió; habló he spoke; salió she went out.

sí, se nos averió yes, it broke down. Why nos? Well, it was *our* car and it let *us* down. Antonio is emphasizing the fact that the breakdown affected them personally – as indeed is the case with most breakdowns!

por eso, llegamos tarde because of this, we arrived late. In Unit 5 you learnt when to use por and when to use para and some of their meanings. Here is another example to add to your list: when you mean 'because of' or 'on account of', use por: por culpa mía, llegué tarde through my own fault, I arrived late. Llegamos: as there is no difference between the endings of the past and present of the first person plural of an -ar verb, llegamos could mean *we arrive* or *we arrived*. You will have to gauge from the context, what tense should be used: llegamos ayer we arrived yesterday; llegamos mañana we arrive tomorrow.

no fue nada grave it was nothing serious. You have learnt fui I went/I was, here now is the third person form usted fue he, she, it, you *went* or he, she, it, *was* or you *were*: fue a casa he went home; ¿fue usted allí? you went there? el tiempo fue muy de prisa time went very quickly; fue médico he was a doctor; fue demasiado temprano para mí it was too early for me.

tuvimos otra we had another one. Tener (to have) has an irregular past tuve, I had; tuve cien pesetas en la mano, I had one hundred pesetas in my hand (see *Grammar* p. 213).

no pudimos encontrar un garaje abierto we couldn't find a garage that was open. Poder (to be able) also has an irregular past rather like tuve above: pude I could.

4 como tenía libre, éste. . . as it was my day off.
Juan is Argentinian and the éste is very much a local variation of eh – a filler word.

y como me atrae mucho la vida al aire libre and as I like the open-air life very much. Atraer = to attract, so what Juan is really saying is that the outdoor life attracts him a great deal. Esa idea me atrae that idea appeals to me.

estuvimos nadando un poco y entreteniéndonos we swam a bit and enjoyed ourselves.

jugando al fútbol playing soccer. If you come across a verb with either -ando or -iendo as an ending you can usually assume that it can be translated into English with the '-ing' form: hablando speaking; comiendo eating; estudiando studying; llegando arriving; llevando carrying; comprando buying etc.

5 *A bus trip to Spain*

Sandra ¿Adónde fue usted de vacaciones el año pasado?

María de los Angeles El año pasado fui de vacaciones a España. Viajé en el autobús directamente desde Londres (hasta) hasta Valencia, (eh . . . pares) paré allí un día y después fui a Cullera, un pueblecito cerca de Valencia. Paré con una amiga y (sencilla . . .) sencillamente, lo pasamos muy descansadas. Y todos los días fuimos a diferentes restaurantes, a probar diferentes platos típicos de la cocina valenciana.

viajé I travelled
paré I stayed
sencillamente simply
probar to try

6 *A trip to Cuenca*

Sandra Bien, ¿hizo usted algún viaje a otro sitio?

María de los Angeles Sí – (fue) fui a Cuenca.

Sandra ¿Y cómo fue a Cuenca – en autobús o coche o tren?

María de los Angeles En tren al ir y volví en autobús.

Sandra ¿Y salió usted muy temprano?

María de los Angeles Sí, muy temprano (para) porque hace mucho calor viajando en la tarde.

7 *Checking flight arrivals*

Pepe Oiga, ¿a qué hora llega el avión de Londres?

Empleado El avión de Londres va a llegar a las cuatro y cuarto – cuatro y quince minutos.

Pepe ¿Trae retraso?

Empleado Pues llega a su hora porque la hora de llegada programada también son las cuatro y quince minutos.

(el) empleado employee
(el) avión plane
programada scheduled

5 ♦ **el año pasado** last year; **la semana pasada** last week; **pasado mañana** the day after tomorrow.

un pueblecito a little village. Note the use of the diminutive **-ito**; you have already come across another example of this **momentito** (a little while). By using the diminutive, Angeles is not only saying that the village was small but also that it had certain 'picture postcard' characteristics: it was quaint.

lo pasamos muy descansadas we spent a very relaxing time
♦ **lo pasamos muy bien** we had a very good time.
pasar = to spend time: **pasé tres días allí** , I spent three days there.

6 ♦ **¿hizo usted algún viaje a otro sitio?** did you make another journey anywhere else? **Hacer** has an irregular past form: **hice** I made/I did; **hice eso ayer**, I made/did that yesterday. **Hizo** (he/she/you made/did) **hizo un viaje muy largo el año pasado**, he/she/you made a long journey last year.

♦ **al ir** on going. **al** + infinitive form of a verb can be literally translated as *on* + verb + *ing*, **al llegar**, on arriving. However, rather than always using the literal translation, use what sounds most natural e.g. **al llegar a casa, escribí una carta** when I arrived home, I wrote a letter.
al coger el tren, perdió el pasaporte as he caught the train, he lost his passport.

7 **¿trae retraso?** is it late, will it be delayed? **(el) retraso** delay.

llega a su hora it's arriving on time.

Key words and phrases

estuve en (Inglaterra)	I was in/went to (England)
hace (dos) años	(two) years ago
fui a (España)	I went to (Spain)
fue a (Italia)	he/she/you went to (Italy)
el año pasado	last year
la semana pasada	last week
pasado mañana	the day after tomorrow
lo pasamos muy bien	we had/we're having a very good time
al llegar	when we arrived
al coger el tren	when we caught the train
¿hizo algún viaje?	did you make any journey?
hice un viaje a . . .	I made a journey to . . .
¿le gustó Cuenca?	did you like Cuenca?
sí, me gustó mucho	yes, I liked it a lot
compré un traje	I bought an outfit/a suit
salí de compras	I went shopping
me perdí	I got lost
llegamos ayer	we arrived yesterday
llegamos mañana	we arrive tomorrow

Practice what you have learned

1 First read the transcript of the conversation below and fill in the blanks with the phrases given in the box. Then listen to the complete dialogue on tape.

New vocabulary:
(**el**) **hermano** brother
(**la**) **hermana** sister
así que so that

Ana María	Y ¿adónde .... el año pasado?
Luis	Pues cerca de Valencia .... que se llama Cullera.
Ana María	Y ¿te gustó?
Luis	¡Oh! sí claro. .... Cullera está cerca del mar, así que pudimos estar en la playa ....
Ana María	Y ¿con quién fuiste?
Luis	Pues con mi familia, ...
Ana María	¿Y cómo fuisteis?
Luis	Pues ...., pero el coche se averió, así que tuvimos que ir en tren – muy temprano a las cinco y media de la mañana .... a eso de las tres de la tarde. Fue un viaje demasiado largo para mi mamá, pero vamos, ... al llegar allí
Ana María	¿Qué te gustó más de Cullera?
Luis	Pues el clima, el mar, la playa, todo eso.
Ana María	Y ¿qué te gustó menos?
Luis	La gente – hay .... en el mediterráneo.

```
todo el día      demasiada gente        decidimos ir en coche
                      fuiste de vacaciones
    mis hermanos y mi hermana menor        pudo descansar
fue estupendo                                       y llegamos allí
          a un pequeño pueblo
```

2 Can you put into Spanish what you did on arrival in Palma? When you have completed the exercise, listen to the tape where you will hear the correct version.

New vocabulary:
coger to catch

Cuando llegué a Palma

a. I arrived in an aeroplane ....

b. I went to the bar ....

c. I wrote two letters ....

d. I went to the toilets ....

e. I had dinner in a restaurant ....

f. I left the airport and caught the bus for Palma

....

3 And now we're in the airport again. Can you guess what the following signs mean? Answers on p. 216

Nada que declarar

Artículos para declarar

Vuelos regulares con destino a Inglaterra

Mostradores de facturación del uno al dieciocho

a. ....

b. ....

c. ....

d. ....

Grammar

The past tense

When talking about actions that took place in the past, you use the past tense.

-ar verbs have the following endings:

comprar   (to buy)

compré	compramos
compraste	comprasteis
compró	compraron

-er and -ir verbs have the following endings:

comer	(to eat)	**escribir**	(to write)
comí	comimos	escribí	escribimos
comiste	comisteis	escribiste	escribisteis
comió	comieron	escribió	escribieron

Some of the most commonly used verbs take an irregular form, though the endings are regular. You have already come across some examples in this unit.

estar	(to be)	**estuve**	I was	
tener	(to have)	**tuve**	I had	**tuve que** . . . I had to . . .
poder	(to be able)	**pude**	I could	
querer	(to want)	**quise**	I wanted	
poner	(to put)	**puse**	I put	
hacer	(to do/make)	**hice**	I did/made	
		hizo (**c** changes to **z** in 3rd person) he/she/ you did/made		

Ir (to go) and **ser** (to be) share the same form in the past tense.

fui (I was/went)	**fuimos**
fuiste (you were/went)	**fuisteis**
fue (he was/went)	**fueron**

1 Write out the correct form of the past for each of the verbs below e.g. Ella (escribir) – escribió.

1 Yo (conseguir) ....

2 Ellos (hablar) ....

3 Nosotros (entrar) ....

4 Vosotros (querer) ....

5 Tú (hacer) ....

6 El (tener) ....

7 Ella (poner) ....

8 Usted (estar) ....

9 Ustedes (poder) ....

Read and understand

Here's a short report from a national newspaper about some Cuban emigrants.

Llegaron a Costa Rica los primeros cubanos

El presidente de Costa Rica fue ayer al aeropuerto para ver a los primeros cubanos que salieron de la Habana. Los cubanos, que llegaron en dos aviones de LACSA, gritaron al bajar del avión ¡Viva Costa Rica! Mucha gente viajó al aeropuerto y recibió a los cubanos con hostilidad. Uno de los aviones se averió en el aeropuerto de la Habana y lo reparon los cubanos emigrantes. Pudieron hacerlo rápidamente y salieron de la Habana con sólo media hora de retraso. Cuando llegaron al aeropuerto de San José en Costa Rica fueron directamente en autobús a un hotel en el centro de la ciudad donde cenaron y hablaron con representantes de la prensa. Todo el día siguiente estuvieron en el hotel con el presidente. Salieron el lunes al pueblecito en donde van a parar durante varios meses . . .

New vocabulary:

gritar to shout
bajar to get off
recibir to receive

(la) hostilidad hostility
(el) representante representative
(la) prensa press

State whether the following statements are true **verdad**, or false **mentira** by ticking the correct boxes. Answers on p. 216.

		verdad	mentira
1	The president's wife went with him to meet the Cuban refugees	☐	☐
2	The Cubans arrived in three Cuban aircraft	☐	☐
3	The Cubans were greeted with insults	☐	☐
4	One of the planes broke down in La Habana	☐	☐
5	It was repaired by the Costa Rican authorities	☐	☐
6	It arrived in Costa Rica a day late	☐	☐

Did you know?

Valencia and the surrounding region

Valencia is the third largest city in Spain and the capital of the Levant region which lies along the eastern coast. The coastal area is a very fertile plain and is famous for its **huertas** (market gardens) particularly those around the city of Valencia. The region itself has many good beaches, good seafood restaurants and a lush climate which has helped produce a fertile rice and orange growing area. The importance of the irrigation system to the area is still in evidence every Thursday when representatives of the various canals meet outside the cathedral in Valencia to sort out their differences. This informal court is called the **Tribunal de las Aguas de Valencia**. There are lots of things to see in the city itself; besides the cathedral, there are a number of churches, the University, the **Lonja de la Seda** (the Silk Exchange), the Plaza del Caudillo, Valencia's main square, and of course dozens of other interesting little **plazas**. Valencia's most important fiesta is of course **Las Fallas** (see Unit 11 p. 159).

Cuenca

Cuenca is another town which is well worth a visit. It has a marvellous old quarter surrounded by two rivers called the Júcar and the Huécar and it is hemmed in on a rocky outcrop between these two rivers. The streets here are very narrow and the houses are arranged higgledy-piggledy, some of them overhanging the river basin below. Because it is so picturesque it has become the home of a number of modern painters and is quite a centre for the arts (a theatre week is held annually). Besides a fine cathedral, it also has a city wall and castle, a famous bridge over the gorge and of course the **casas colgadas** or hanging houses.

Your turn to speak

Now it's up to you to practise the past tense. You will be talking about your holidays in Spain last July; Isabel will prompt you.

And finally   Now listen to the dialogues again and test yourself on the *Key words and phrases*. Go through the past tense on p. 213 and try to memorize all the irregular pasts listed on the page as these are the ones that you are most likely to need.

You should now have a good basic knowledge of Spanish and the ability to cope in most of the situations that you are likely to have to face while on holiday – an ability that will improve with practice. ¡**Suerte!**

Revision/Review

Now turn to p. 220 and complete the revision sections on Units 11–15. On tape the revision section follows straight after this unit.

Answers

Practice what you have learned p. 212 Exercise 3 (a) nothing to declare (b) articles to declare (c) scheduled flights to England (d) check-in desks 1 – 18.

Grammar p. 213 Exercise 1 (**1**) conseguí. (**2**) hablaron. (**3**) entramos. (**4**) quisisteis. (**5**) hiciste. (**6**) tuvo. (**7**) puso. (**8**) estuvo. (**9**) pudieron.

Read and understand p. 214 (**1**) mentira. (**2**) mentira. (**3**) verdad. (**4**) verdad. (**5**) mentira. (**6**) mentira.

Revision/Review   Units 1 – 5

Review is vital. Before you go on to Unit 6, we suggest you first:

1 Play through all the dialogues from Units 1 – 5 reading them aloud from the book at the same time.
2 Reread the *Grammar* notes from these units.
3 Make sure you know the *Key phrases* from these units.
4 Do the following exercises. They have been designed to help you review, so do look back through Units 1 – 5 as much as you like.
5 Do the revision exercise which follows straight after Unit 5 on tape. This is similar to the ones in the sections *Your turn to speak*, so you won't need your book.

2 You're at a hotel reception. The answers to the receptionist's questions have been given to you. Can you translate them into Spanish? When you have completed the exercises, turn on your cassette for the complete dialogue.

Recepcionista Buenas tardes.
Julia Good afternoon. Have you a room free?

....

Recepcionista Sí. ¿Para una o dos noches?
Julia For two nights please.

....

Recepcionista Bien. Nombre por favor.
Julia Julia Smith.

....

Recepcionista ¿Casada o soltera?
Julia Married.

....

Recepcionista ¿De dónde?
Julia From England.

....

Recepcionista Muy bien. Pasaporte por favor.
Julia Here you are.

....

3 You're in a bar ordering a drink and an ice-cream. Some words are missing from the conversation; given the context, can you work out what they might be? When you have finished the exercise, listen to the tape where you will hear the complete dialogue.

Camarero   Sí señora ¿qué desea?

Cliente   Un .... por favor.

Camarero   Bien. Hay de café y de caramelo.

Cliente   .... caramelo por favor. Y un

       ....

Camarero   ¿Solo o con ....?

Cliente   Solo. ¿Hay un banco por ....?

Camarero   Sí, al otro .... de la Plaza Mayor.

Cliente   ¿Está ....?

Camarero   No, muy...Coge usted la primera

       bocacalle a la derecha y allí ....

Cliente   ¿Tengo que ir .... recto?

Camarero   Sí, hasta la primera bocacalle.

Cliente   Gracias y ¿... es todo?

Camarero   Ciento cincuenta pesetas, señora.

Revision/Review   Units 6 – 10

2 You are in a shop buying a souvenir. Listen to the conversation on tape as many times as you need and then turn the machine off and answer the following questions. (Answers at foot of page.)

a. How much do the headscarves cost? ....

b. What colour plates does the shop have? ....

c. What is special about them? ....

d. What remark does the sales assistant make about the mantillas? ....

e. What are the headscarves made of? ....

3 On tape you will hear a woman buying a train ticket. Tick the items below if they are what she wants. (Answers at foot of page.)

☐ ida
☐ 750 pts
☐ Córdoba
☐ 1°
☐ 2°
☐ ida y vuelta
☐ Granada
☐ 850 pts

Answers

Exercise (2) (a) between 3000 and 5000 pesetas (b) red, green and blue (c) made by hand (d) she only has mantillas in black (e) crepe, polyester and cotton.

Exercise 3 you should have ticked: Córdoba, second class, return ticket and 850 pesetas.

Revision/Review   Units 11 – 15

1 On tape you will hear Ana describing what she will be doing tomorrow. Listen as often as you need and then switch the tape off and list the things she will be doing below *in English*. You'll find that there are ten. (Answers at foot of page)

a. ....

b. ....

c. ....

d. ....

e. ....

f. ....

g. ....

h. ....

i. ....

j. ....

2 Here's a day in the life of Miguel. The pictures tell you what he does – can you complete the sentences. (We've done **f.** for you as an example.) When you have finished the exercise, listen to the tape where you will hear the answers.

a. Me levanto a las ocho ....

b. Me visto a las nueve ....

c. Me arreglo a las diez y media ....

d. Regreso a las dos ....

e. Voy a mi habitación a las cuatro ....

f. Salgo a las cinco para visitar el pueblo

g. Me voy a la cama a las once ....

Answers

1 (**a**) she'll go to the beach (**b**) have breakfast in a bar (**c**) she'll swim (**d**) she'll play with her sisters (**e**) she'll return to the hotel to have lunch (**f**) she'll have a siesta (**g**) she'll go again to the beach (**h**) she'll go out for a walk (**i**) she'll return to the hotel (**j**) she'll go to bed at 11.30/midnight.

Grammar summary

For easy reference the most useful grammar points are set out below.

Grammatical terms

The basic rules

Grammatical terms	The basic rules
A VERB denotes action or being e.g. the man *goes*; I *am* Mary *hates* football	There are three main groups of regular verbs **1** those with infinitives which end in **-ar** e.g. **hablar, terminar** (see Unit 1, p. 17) **2** those with infinitives ending in **-er** e.g. **vender, beber** (see Unit 2, p. 31) **3** those with infinitives ending in **-ir** e.g. **vivir, escribir** (see Unit 3, p. 45)
The INFINITIVE is the form of the verb preceded in English by 'to' e.g. *to go; to be; to hate*	Unfortunately, some of the most commonly used verbs are irregular and you need to learn these individually. The present tenses of irregular verbs given in this course are: **ser** (Unit 1), **tener** (Unit 2), **saber, conocer, poder** (Unit 8), **hacer** (Unit 7) and **salir** (Unit 13).
The SUBJECT of the verb is the person or thing who acts or is,. e.g. *the man* goes; *I* am; *Mary* hates football	Remember that simple present tenses such as **yo hablo** can be translated in two ways. EITHER 'I am speaking' or 'I speak' But in Spanish it's more usual to omit the subject: **hablo** (I speak) is more common than **yo hablo** (I speak).
The OBJECT of the verb is the person or thing on the receiving end – e.g. Mary hates *football*; John hates *it*; Mary loves *him*	As well as saying what are you doing, you need to be able to talk about what you have done (in the *past*) and what are going to do (in the *future*). *The past tense*, known as the *preterite*, is explained in Unit 15. This tense is formed by adding the appropriate endings to the 'root' of the verb – the main part of the verb, e.g. **compré; comí**. In the negative, this becomes **no compré; no comí**. Some preterites are irregular. There is a list of these on p. 213. There is also another *past tense*, called the *imperfect*. You are not expected to learn it at this stage, but it does occur in some of the later dialogues. You can express *future* intentions in two ways **1** by saying *I am going to*. Use the present tense of **ir** + the infinitive of the relevant verb e.g. **voy a venir**. **2** by using the *future* tense. This is formed by adding the appropriate endings to the infinitive of the verb e.g. **compraré, comeré, viviré**. Ways of expressing the future are outlined in Unit 14. When two verbs follow each other, the second one is always in the infinitive, e.g. **voy a ir a España; pienso salir**.
A NOUN is the name of a person or thing e.g. *James, child, dog, book*	All Spanish nouns are either masculine or feminine. To form their plurals add an **s** or **es** if the noun ends in a consonant **libro libros; ciudad ciudades**
The ARTICLES in English are *the, a, an*, and *some*.	The word for 'the' before a masculine singular noun is **el** and before a masculine plural one **los**. The word for 'the' before a feminine singular noun is **la** and before a feminine plural noun **las** e.g. **el libro, los libros, la carta, las cartas**. The word for 'a', 'an' is **un** before a masculine noun and **una** before a feminine one, e.g. **un libro, una carta**

An ADJECTIVE describes a noun or pronoun – e.g. *beautiful, green, small, comfortable*	In Spanish, an adjective 'agrees' with the noun or pronoun it describes, i.e. it is feminine when describing something feminine and plural when describing something plural. Plurals are formed in the same way as the plurals of nouns (see above) – generally by adding **-s**. If the adjective ends in a vowel e.g. **hermoso**, simply add an **-s**, **hermoso** and **-es** if the adjective ends in a consonant e.g. **inglés, ingleses.** As a general rule masculine adjectives end in **o**, **hermoso** and feminine adjectives in **a**, **hermosa**. If the adjective ends in a consonant, its ending remains the same e.g. **un hombre feliz, una mujer feliz.** Some adjectives shorten their form if placed before their noun **un gran hombre** a great man **un hombre grande** a large man But most adjectives are placed after the noun they describe.
An ADVERB describes the way something happens, e.g. *well, quickly, beautifully* in 'She reads *well*', 'She runs *quickly*', and 'She sings *beautifully*'.	These are formed by adding **-mente** to the feminine singular of the adjective **estupendo estupendamente** or if there is no feminine form, the masculine singular **feliz felizmente** Some adverbs are irregular **bien** well, **mejor** better, **mal** badly, **temprano** early, **bastante** fairly, rather
PREPOSITIONS in English are such words as *near, by, to, for, with, over through* and *into*	The two most common prepositions in Spanish are **de** (from, of) and **a** (to, at) e.g. **soy de Londres** I am from London **la maleta de María** Maria's suitcase **voy a Madrid** I am going to Madrid **De** and **a** change their form before **el** to **del: la casa del dueño** the boss's house and **al: voy al bar** I'm going to the bar If the object is a person, then you need to add **a** e.g. **veo a Juan** I see Juan

A PRONOUN stands for a noun e.g. 'Mary loves Fred – *she* loves *him*.' *She* is a subject pronoun and *him* is an object pronoun.
Pronouns can refer to people or things, e.g. 'The man frightened the children – *he* frightened *them*'; 'The cars damaged the lawn – *they* damaged *it*.'
	The subject pronouns are **yo, tu, el, ella nosotros (as), vosotros (as), ellos, ellas. Usted** and **ustedes** are used for the formal *you.* You do not need to express the subject pronoun – it is understood from the form of the verb
	  canto I sing
	  baila he dances, she dances

	The object pronouns are as follows **me lleva** he takes me **te lleva** he takes you **lo lleva** he takes it (m.) **la lleva** he takes it (f.) **le lleva** he takes him, her **nos lleva** he takes us **os lleva** he takes you **las lleva** he takes them (fp.) **los lleva** he takes them (mp.) **les lleva** he takes them There is some discussion about the use of **la, le** and **lo** and **los, las** and **les**. A simple rule is to use **lo(s)** and **la(s)** when referring to masculine and feminine things and **le(s)** for men and **la(s)** for women.

Some verbs take an 'indirect' object rather than a 'direct' object e.g. 'he speaks *to* me' not 'he speaks *me*.'	The only difference between indirect and direct objects is in the third person form (*he, it*). Use **le** when saying 'to her, to him, to it or to you (**usted**)' and **les** for 'to them or to you (**ustedes**)' **le habla** he speaks to him/to her/ to it/ to you (**usted**). **les habla** he speaks to them/to you (**ustedes**) If you want to avoid ambiguity, add **a él, a ella, a Vd., a ellos, a ellas, a Vds.** **les doy el libro a ellos** I give them the book (masculine plural) **les doy el libro a ellas** I give them the book (feminine plural)
POSSESSIVE ADJECTIVES are words like *my, your* and *his*.	Possessive adjectives in Spanish are as follows **mi casa** my house **mis casas** my houses **tu casa** your house **tus casas** your houses **su casa** his, her, your house **sus casas** his, her, your houses **nuestra casa** our house **nuestras casas** our houses **vuestra casa** your house **vuestras casas** your houses **su casa** their, your house **sus casas** their, your houses When talking about parts of the body or clothes, Spaniards use the definite article rather than the possessive adjective **tengo el pelo negro** I have black hair

Numbers

1	uno	31	treinta y uno (a)
2	dos	32	treinta y dos
3	tres	33	treinta y tres
4	cuatro	34	treinta y cuatro
5	cinco	35	treinta y cinco
6	seis	36	treinta y seis
7	siete	37	treinta y siete
8	ocho	38	treinta y ocho
9	nueve	39	treinta y nueve
10	diez	40	cuarenta
11	once	43	cuarenta y tres
12	doce	48	cuarenta y ocho
13	trece	50	cincuenta
14	catorce	51	cincuenta y uno (a)
15	quince	59	cincuenta y nueve
16	dieciséis	60	sesenta
17	diecisiete	63	sesenta y tres
18	dieciocho	67	sesenta y siete
19	diecinueve	70	setenta
20	veinte	72	setenta y dos
21	veintiuno (a)	80	ochenta
22	veintidós	90	noventa
23	veintitrés	100	ciento (cien)
24	veinticuatro	105	ciento cinco
25	veinticinco	200	doscientos (as)
26	veintiséis	300	trescientos (as)
27	veintisiete	400	cuatrocientos (as)
28	veintiocho	500	quinientos (as)
29	veintinueve	600	seiscientos (as)
30	treinta	700	setecientos (as)
		1000	mil

1 – 100

Only those numbers ending in **-uno** have a masculine and feminine form; they do not have a plural form.

veintiún hombres
veintiuna mujeres

Note that as in the above case, if **veintiuno** comes before a noun it is shortened to **veintiún**. However, if the number stands alone you should use the full form.

¿cuántos hombres? veintiuno.
¿cuántas mujeres? veintiuna.

100

Ciento becomes **cien** when you are talking about exactly 100 objects.

cien casas one hundred houses
cien gramos one hundred grammes
ciento cincuenta gramos one hundred and fifty grammes

200 – 900

These numbers have masculine and feminine forms
doscientos chicos two hundred boys
doscientas niñas two hundred girls

1000

Mil does not change its form
mil novecientos ochenta y dos 1982

Grammar in the course

Vocabulary

The feminine ending of adjectives is given in brackets e.g. **abierto(a)** means that the masculine is **abierto** and the feminine **abierta**. Where nothing is given in brackets, the feminine form is the same as the masculine, e.g. **canadiense**.

a to, at, on; **a las . . . at . . .** o'clock
abajo below
abierto (a) open
abonado (a) subscriber
abonar to subscribe
abrazo (m.) hug
abril (m.) April
abrir to open
acabar to finish; **acabar de** to have just finished
acampar to camp
aceite (m.) oil
aceituna (f.) olive
acomodadora (f.) usherette
aconsejar to advise
acostarse to go to bed
actividad (f.) activity
acto (m.) function
acuerdo (m.) agreement; **de acuerdo** OK
adelante forward; **¡adelante!** come in
además besides
adiós goodbye
¿adónde? where (to)?
aduanero (m.) customs' officer
adulto (m.) adult
aeropuerto (m.) airport
Africa(f.) Africa
afuera outside; **las afueras** the outskirts
agencia inmobiliaria (f.) estate agent's
agobiado (a) worn out
agosto (m.) August
agradable pleasant, agreeable
agua (f.) water; **agua mineral** mineral water
ahora now
aire (m.) air; **aire libre** open air
Alemania (f.) Germany
algo anything, something
algodón (m.) cotton
algún, alguno (a) any, some
almorzar to lunch
almuerzo(m.) lunch
altura (f.) height; **hasta la altura de** as far as
alumna (f.) pupil (girl)
alumno (m.) pupil (boy)
allí there; **allí mismo** right there
ambiente (m.) atmosphere
ambos(as) both
americano, (a) American
amigo (a) friend
andaluz (a) Andalucian
andar to walk
andén (m.) platform
animal (m.) animal
antes de before
antigüedades (f.) antiques
año (m.) year **¿cuántos años tiene?** how old are you?

aparcar to park
apartado de correos (m.) box number
apartamento (m.) flat
apellido(m.) surname
apetecer to feel like
aprovechar; ¡qué aproveche! enjoy your meal!
aproximadamente approximately
aquí here; **por aquí** around here
ardor (m.); ardor de estómago heart burn
aroma (m.) scent
arreglado (a) ready
arreglarse to get oneself ready
arriba above
artículo (m.) article
asado (a) roast
así like this; **así que** so that
atender to look after
Atlántico (m.) the Atlantic
atraer to attract
atrás behind
atravesar to cross
atún (m.) tuna fish
autobús (m.) bus
autocar (m.) coach
autopista (f.) motorway
autoservicio (m.) self-service
avenida (f.) avenue
avería (f.) breakdown
averiarse to breakdown
avión (m.) aeroplane
ayuntamiento (m.) town hall
azafata (f.) air hostess
azul blue; **azul marino** navy blue

bacalao (m.) salt cod; **bacalao a la vizcaína** Vizcayan salted cod
bailar to dance
bajar to go down
bajo (a) short; **planta baja** ground floor
balón (m.) ball
banco (m.) bank; **tarjeta de banco (f.)** banker's card
baño (m.) bath
bar (m.) bar
barato (a) cheap
barbaridad (f.) a lot; **¡qué barbaridad!** how awful!
barco (m.) ship
barra (f.) loaf
barrio (m.) neighbourhood
bastante enough
batista (f.) batiste
beber to drink
beige beige
beso (m.) kiss
bicicleta (f.) bicycle; **montar en bicicleta** to ride a bicycle
bien well; **más bien** rather; **muy**

bien very good, very well
bifurcación (f.) junction
billete (m.) ticket
blanco(a) white
blazer (m.) blazer
boca (f.) mouth; bocacalle (f.) entrance
  to street, intersection
bocadillo (m.) sandwich
bolsa (f.) bag
bonito (a) pretty
bordo; a bordo on board
bota (f.) boot
botella (f.) bottle
botellín (m.) small bottle (of beer)
brisa (f.) breeze
británico (a) British
bronceador (m.) suntan lotion
bueno (a) good
burdeos maroon
buscar to look for
butaca (f.) stall (in theatre)

caballero (m.) gentleman;
  caballeros gents (toilets)
cabeza (f.) head
cabo; al cabo de at the end of
cabra (f.) goat
cada each
caer to fall
café (m.) coffee; café solo black coffee
caja (f.) box, cash desk
calamares squid; calamares fritos fried
  squid
calefacción (f.) heating
calidad (f.) quality
calor (m.) heat; hace calor it's hot
caluroso(a) hot
calle (f.) street
cama (f.) bed
camarero (a) waiter/steward, waitress
cambiar to change
cambio (m.) change
camino (m.) way, path, road
camisa (f.) shirt
camiseta (f.) tee-shirt
camping (m.) campsite
canadiense Canadian
cansado (a) tired
cantidad (f.) quantity
caña (f.) glass
capacidad (f.) capacity
cara (f.) face
caramelo (m.) sweet
caravana (f.) caravan
carne (f.) meat
carnet de camping/identidad
  (m.) camping/identity card
caro (a) expensive, carísimo very
  expensive
carretera (f.) main road
carta (f.) letter
cartel (m.) poster
casa (f.) house; casa de
  huéspedes guest house
casado (a) married
catedral (f.) cathedral

categoría (f.) category, class
catorce fourteen
cena (f.) dinner; cenar to dine
centro (m.) centre
cerca near
cero zero
cerrarse to be closed
cerveza (f.) beer
cien hundred
cigarrillo (m.) cigarette
cilíndrico (a) cylindrical
cinco five
cincuenta fifty
cincuenta y cinco fifty-five
cine (m.) cinema
circular circular
ciudad (f.) city
claro (a) clear, of course
clase (f.) class, kind, sort
clásico (a) classic
cliente (m.) customer
clima (m.) climate
club náutico (m.) sailing club
cobrar to cover, charge
cocina (f.) kitchen; cocina
  amueblada fitted kitchen
cocinar to cook
coche (m.) car
cochinillo (m.) suckling pig
coger to get, catch
colegio (m.) secondary school (private)
color (m.) colour
comedor (m.) dining-room
comenzar to begin
comida (f.) meal
¿cómo? how, pardon?
como as, like; como de costumbre as
  usual
cómodo comfortable
complementar to complement
completo (a) complete
compra (f.) purchase hacer su
  compra to make your purchase
comprar to buy
comprender to understand, to include
comprimido (m.) pill, tablet
comprobar to check
con with; conmigo with me;
  contigo with you
condición (f.) condition; en buenas
  condiciones in good conditions
conocer to know
conocido (a) known
conseguir to obtain
consomé (m.) clear soup
construir to build; construído (a) built
contentísimo (a) very happy
conveniente advisable/desirable
correos post office
correr to run; echar a correr to break
  into a run
corrida (f.) bullfight
cortar to cut
cosa (f.) thing
coser to sew
costa (f.) coast

costar to cost
creer to believe, think
crema (f.) cream
crepe (m.) crêpe material
cruce (m.) crossroads
cruzar to cross
¿cuál? which, what?
cualquier (a) any
cuando when
¿cuándo? when?
¿cuánto? ¿cuán? how much, how many?
cuarenta forty
cuarenta y cinco forty-five
cuarto (m.) a quarter; menos cuarto a quarter to; y cuarto quarter past
cuarto de baño (m.) bathroom
cuatro four
cubano (a) Cuban
cubierto (a) covered
cuenta (f.) bill
cuero (m.) leather
cuestión (f.) question
culpa (f.) fault
cumpleaños (m.) birthday
cupón (m.) form
cuyo (a) whose, of whom, of which

champú (m.) shampoo
chandal (m.) track suit
chaqueta (f.) jacket
cheque de viaje (m.) travellers' cheque
cheviot (m.) type of woollen cloth
chico (m.) boy
chica (f.) girl
chocolate (m.) chocolate
chorizo (m.) spicy sausage
churro (m.) type of fritter/doughnut

dar to give; dar un paseo to go for a walk; dar clases to teach
de of, from
deber to have to, to owe
decir to say
dejar to leave
delante (de) in front of
demasiado too much
dentro inside
depender (de) to depend on
dependiente (m.) sales assistant
deportes (m.) sport
derecha right a la derecha on the right
desayunar to have breakfast
desayuno (m.) breakfast
descanso (m.) rest
desde from
desear to wish for
despacio slowly
despejado (a) clear
después afterwards
desviarse to turn
detestar to hate
día (m.) day; buenos días good morning; el día del santo Saint's day
diario (a) daily
diciembre (m.) December

diecinueve nineteen
dieciocho eighteen
dieciséis sixteen
diecisiete seventeen
diez ten
diferencia (f.) difference
difícil difficult
dinero (m.) money
discoteca (f.) dicothèque
distinto (a) different
divertirse to enjoy oneself
doblar to turn
doce twelve
docena (f.) dozen
documento (m.) document
dolor (m.) pain; dolor de estómago stomach ache
domicilio (m.) home
domingo Sunday
don Mr.
doña Mrs
donde where; ¿dónde? where?
dorado (a) golden
dormitorio (m.) bedroom
doscientos (as) two hundred
ducha (f.) shower
dulce sweet
duración (f.) length
durante during
durar to last
duro (m.) five pesetas
duro (a) hard

echar to throw; echar a correr to break into a run; echar una siesta to have a siesta; echarse a reír to burst out laughing
edad (f.) age ¿qué edad tiene? how old are you?
efectivamente precisely
el the
él he, him
elección (f.) election
electrotrén (m.) electric train
ella she, her, it
ellos (as) they, them
empleada (f.) employee (female)
empleado (m.) employee (male)
en in
encantado (a) delighted
encantar to delight
encargarse to take charge of
encima (de) on top of; por encima de over
encontrar to find, to meet
encontrarse to be found
enfrente (de) in front of/opposite
enero (m.) January
ensaladilla (f.) Russian salad
entonces so, then
entrar to enter, go in
entregar to hand over
entremeses (mp.) hors d'oeuvres
entretener to amuse
enviar to send
época (f.) time

escribir to write
ese (a) that
esmalte (m.) nail polish
eso that
esos (as) those
España Spain
español(a) Spanish
especialmente especially
especificar to specify
esperar to wait (for)
esposo (m.) husband
esposa (f.) wife
establecimiento (m.) establishment
estación (f.) station, season
estampado (a.) printed
estanco (m.) tobacconist's
estar to be ¿cómo estás? how are you?
    está bien OK, fine
este (m.) east
este (a) this
éste (a) this one
estilo (m.) style
esto this
estos (as) these
éstos (as) these (ones)
estrella (f.) star
estudiante (m. and f.) student
estupendo(a) marvellous
eterno (a) eternal
expreso (m.) express train
extenderse to extend, to spread out
extensión (f.) extension
extra large, 98 octane (petrol)
extremo (a) extreme
extremo (m.) end

faena (f.) task
falda (f.) skirt
fantasía (f.) whim, fancy
farmacia (f.) chemist shop
farmacéutica (f.) chemist, pharmacist
favorito (a) favourite
febrero (m.) February
fecha (f.) date
ferrocarril (m.) railway
festivo (a) festive; día festivo public
    holiday
fijo (a) fixed; precio fijo fixed price
final (m.) end; al final de at the end of
fino fine
firma (f.) signature
flan (m.) cream caramel
fonda (f.) inn, pub
formar to form
francés (a) French
freír to fry
frecuencia (f.) frequency, con
    frecuencia frequently
fresa (f.) strawberry
frío (a) cold; hace frío it's cold
frito (a) fried; calamares fritos fried
    squid
fruta (f.) fruit
a la fuerza willy-nilly, against one's will
fútbol (m.) football

gallego (a) person from Galicia
gamba (f.) prawn
ganar to win, to earn
garaje (m.) garage
garrafa (f.) carafe
gas (m.) con gas fizzy; sin gas still
gasolinera (f.) service station
gasolinero (a) service station attendant
gazpacho (m.) spicy cold tomato soup
gente (f.) people
girar to turn
girasol (m.) sunflower; aceite de
    girasol sunflower oil
gobierno (m.) government
golfista (m. and f.) golfer
gordo (a) fat
gracias (f.) thanks; muchas
    gracias thanks very much
grado (m.) degree
gramo (m.) gramme
gran, grande big, large
grave serious
gris grey
gritar to shout
grueso (a) thick
gustar to like; ¿te gusta? do you like
    (it)?; no me gusta I don't like (it)
gusto (m.) taste; tanto gusto so pleased
    to meet you

habitación (f.) room, bedroom
hablar to talk
hacer to do, to make; no me hace
    gracia I don't like (it); hacer la
    cama to make the bed; hacer las
    maletas to pack suitcases
hacia towards
hasta up to, as far as
hay there is, there are; hay que you've
    got to
helado (m.) ice-cream
hija (f.) daughter
hijo (m.) son; hijos (mp.) children
histórico (a) historic
hoja (f.) de reclamaciones complaints
    form
¡hola! hallo
hombre (m.) man; ¡hombre! good
    heavens!
hora (f.) hour; ¿qué hora es? what
    time is it?; a su hora on time
horario (m.) timetable
horizontal across (crosswords)
hostal (m.) hostel
hostilidad (f.) hostility, aggression
hotel (m.) hotel
hoy today
huevo (m.) egg

ida (f) outward journey; ida y
    vuelta return journey
idioma (m.) language
igual the same
imitación (f.) imitation
imperdible (m.) pin, safety pin
importante important

impuestos (mp.) taxes
incomparable incomparable
indicador (m.) sign
ingeniero (m.) engineer
Inglaterra (f.) England
inglés (a) English
invierno (m.) winter
ir to go; ir de tiendas to go shopping; ir
   de paseo to go for a walk
isla (f.) island; islas Baleares the
   Balearic islands
itinerario (m.) journey, itinerary
izquierda left; a la izquierda on the left

jamón (m.) ham; jamón
   serrano smoked ham
jarabe (m.) syrup
jardín (m.) garden
jefe (m. and f.) chief, boss; jefe de
   sección departmental manager
jubilado (a) retired
jueves (m.) Thursday
jugar to play
juguete (m.) toy
julio (m.) July
junio (m.) June
junto (a) together
justo(a) just, exactly; cien pesetas
   justas one hundred pesetas exactly

kilo (m.) kilo
kilómetro (m.) kilometre

la the, it, her
lado (m.) side al lado de by the side of
lápiz (m.) pencil
largo (a) long
lata (f.) tin
lavabo (m.) washbasin
lavar to wash; lavarse to wash oneself
leche (f.) milk
lechuga (f.) lettuce
leer to read
lejos far away
lengua (f.) tongue, language
les (to) you, (to) them
levantarse to get up
libre free; ¿queda libre? are you free?
libro (m.) book
ligeramente lightly
limpiar to clean
liquidar to liquidate, to get rid of
litro (m.) litre
lo the, that which, it, him, lo
   que which, what
localidad (f.) cinema or theatre seat
Londres London
luces de tráfico (fp.) traffic lights
luego then, later
lugar (m.) place
lujoso (a) luxury
lunes (m.) Monday

llamada (f.) call
llamar to call, phone; llamarse to be
called; ¿cómo se llama? what is your
   name?
llegada (f.) arrival
llegar to arrive
llover to rain
lluvioso (a) rainy
lluvia (f.) rain

magnetófono (m.) tape recorder
maíz (m.) maize; aceite de maíz maize
   oil
mal badly; malo (a) bad; malas
   digestiones indigestion
maleta (f.) suitcase; hacer la maleta to
   pack a suitcase
manchego (a) from La Mancha
manicura (f.) manicure
mano (f.) hand
mantilla (f.) mantilla
mañana tomorrow; pasado
   mañana the day after tomorrow; por
   la mañana in the morning
mar (m.) sea
marca (f.) brand
marcar to dial
marcharse to go
marfil (m.) ivory; marfil tallado carved
   ivory
marisco (m.) shellfish
marrón brown
martes (m.) Tuesday
marzo (m.) March
más more, most, else, plus; ¿algo
   más? anything else? más bien rather
matrimonio (m.) married couple; cama
   de matrimonio (f.) double bed;
   habitación de matrimonio double
   room
mayo (m.) May
mayor eldest, older, grown up; La Plaza
   Mayor Main Square
mayormente chiefly, especially
medicina (f.) medicine
médico (m.) doctor
medida (f.) measurement, size
medio (a) half; medio aseo (m.) shower
   room media hora half an hour; las
   dos y media half past two
mediodía (m.) midday
mejor better, best
melocotón (m.) peach
menos less; las doce menos
   veinte twenty to twelve
mentira(f.) lie; false
menú (m.) menu
merendar to have tea; merienda (f.) tea
merluza (f.) hake; merluza a la
   romana hake fried in batter
mes (m.) month
mesa (f.) table
metro (m.) metre
metro (m.) underground
mi my
mí me
miércoles Wednesday
mil thousand

minuto (m.) minute
mío (a) my
mirar to look at
mismo (a) same, very
moldeadora (f.) soft perm
moneda (f.) change
montaña (f.) mountain
montañoso (a) mountainous
montar en bicicleta to ride a bicycle
mortadela (f.) kind of Italian sausage
mostrador (m.) de facturación check in
    counter (at airport)
mostrar to show
mujer (f.) woman, wife
murallas (fp.) city walls
muy very

nacional national; la nacional uno name
    of a road, i.e. NI
nacionalidad (f.) nationality
nada nothing; de nada you're welcome
nadar to swim
naranja (f.) orange
naturalmente of course
necesario (a) necessary
necesitar to need
negro (a) black
nevar to snow
ni . . . ni neither, nor
nieto (a) grandson, grand-daughter
nieve (f.) snow
niño (a) boy, girl
nivel (m.) level
no no, not
noche (f.) night
nombre (m.) name
normal normal
normalmente usually
norte north; al norte in the north, to
    the north
nos (to) us
nosotros (as) we, us
novecientos (as) nine hundred
novedad (f.) novelty
noventa ninety
noviembre (m.) November
novillada (f.) a bullfight for trainee
    bullfighters
novio (a) boyfriend, girlfriend, fiancé
    (e)
nube (f) cloud; nubes
    alternas occasional clouds
nubloso (a) cloudy
nuboso (a) cloudy
nueve nine
número number
nunca never

o or
octubre (m.) October
ochenta eighty
ocho eight
odiar (m.) to hate
oeste (m.) west
oferta (f.) offer
oficina (f.) office; oficina de

turismo tourist office
oir to hear
ojo (m.) eye ¡ojo! look out!
oliva (f.) olive; aceite de oliva olive oil
oro (m.) gold
oscilar to oscilate, to vary
otoño (m.) autumn
otro (a) other
oveja (f.) sheep

padre (m.) father
paella (f.) paella
pagar to pay
país (m.) country
paisaje (m.) countryside
palco (m.) box (in a theatre)
pan (m.) bread
pantalones (mp.) trousers, pants
pañuelo (m.) handkerchief, scarf
paquete (m.) packet
par (m.) pair; par de zapatos pair of
    shoes
para for, to
parabrisas (m.) windscreen
parada (f.) stop; parada de
    autobuses bus stop
parador (m.) state run hotel
paraíso (m.) paradise
parar to stop
parecer to seem; me parece que . . . I
    think that . . . ¿qué le parece? what
    do you think of . . .?
parque (m.) park; parque
    infantil playground
parte (f.) part
participar to participate
partido (m.) match; partido de
    fútbol football match
pasar to spend (time); pasadas dos
    horas after two hours
pasaporte (m.) passport
pasear to go for a walk
paseo (m.) walk dar un paseo/ir de
    paseo to go for a walk
patata (f.) potato
peaje (m.) toll
pedir to ask for
peinarse to do one's hair
película (f.) film
pelota (f.) ball
peluquero (a) hairdresser
pensar to think
pensión (f.) guest house
peor worst, worse
pequeño(a) small
perderse to lose oneself
perfecto (a) perfect;
    perfectamente exactly
perfumería (f.) perfumery
periódico (m.) newspaper
período (m.) period
pero but
persona (f.) person
pescado (m.) fish
peseta (f.) peseta
peso (m.) weight

picante spicy
pie (m.) foot; a pie on foot
piel (f.) skin
pila (f.) battery
piscina (f.) swimming pool
piso (m.) floor, flat; el primer piso the
  first floor
planchar to iron
planta (f.) floor; primera planta first
  floor
plata (f.) silver
plateado (a) silvery
plato (m.) plate, course; de primer
  plato as a first course; plato
  combinado one course meal
playa (f.) beach
plaza (f.) square
poder to be able to; se puede one can;
  no se puede one cannot
poliester (m.) polyester
polipiel (f.) synthetic leather
poner to put; ponerse de acuerdo to
  agree on
por along, by, for; por
  ahí roundabouts; por aquí around
  here; por ciento per cent; por
  favor please; por encima de over,
  above
porque because
¿por qué? why?
posible possible
postre (m.) dessert; de postre for
  dessert
potable drinkable
precio (m.) price; a precio fijo at a fixed
  price
precioso (a) lovely
preferir to prefer
prensa (f.) press
preparado (a.) prepared, ready
presidente (m.) president
presión (f.) pressure
primavera (f.) spring
primero (a) first; de primer plato as a
  first course
probar to try on
procedencia (f.) point of departure
procedente de from;
procedente de Madrid from Madrid
profesor (a) teacher
programa (m.) programme
programado (a) scheduled
propio (a) own, special
provincia (f.) province
pueblo (m.) village
puente (m.) bridge
puerto (m.) port
pues well
punto, en punto on time

que that, which
¿qué? what? which?
quedar to be; quedarse to stay, to
  remain
querer to want, wish; querer decir to
  mean; quisiera I would like

queso (m.) cheese
quien who
¿quién? who?
quince fifteen
quinientos (as) five hundred
quinqué (m;) lamp

ración (f.) portion
rápido (m.) express train
rápido (a) fast
raqueta (f.) raquet
rato (m.) while; dentro de un rato in a
  while
realmente really
rebajado (a) reduced
recargo (m.) surcharge; hacer un
  recargo to make an extra charge
recepción (f.) reception desk
recibir to receive
recogida (f.) collection
recomendar to recommend
recto (a) straight; todo recto straight on
recuerdo (m.) souvenir
reflejo (m.) reflection; reflejos
  colorantes highlights
refrigerio (m.) cold drink, snack
región (f.) region
regional regional
regresar to return
regular regular; ¿cómo estás?
  regular how are you? so so
reina (f.) queen
reír to laugh; echarse a reír to burst
  out laughing
relajante relaxing
reloj (m.) watch
rellenar to fill in
reparar to repair
retirar to collect
retraso (m.) delay
retrete (m.) lavatory
revitalizante (m.) conditioner
rey (m.) king
río (m.) river
rojo (a) red
romano (a) Roman
ropa (f.) clothes
rubio (a) blond
rueda (f.) wheel; rueda de
  repuesto spare wheel

sábado (m.) Saturday
saber to know no sé I don't know
sacar to take out, to get
sal (f.) salt
salida (f.) exit
salir to go out salir de compras to go
  shopping
salón (m.) sitting-room
santo (a) saint el día del santo saint's
  day
sardina (f.) sardine
se one, oneself
sea; o sea that is to say
secadora de mano (f.) hairdrier
sección (f.) department

seco (a) dry
seda (f.) silk; **seda natural** natural silk
seguida; **en seguida** at once, right away
seguido; **todo seguido** straight on
seguir to contine, to follow
según according to
segundo (a) second; **de segundo** as
 second course
seguro (a) sure, certain
seis six
selva (f.) forest
semana (f.) week
semi directo (m.) stopping train
sencillamente simply
sencillo (a) simple; **habitación
 sencilla** single room
sentido (m.) direction
sentir to feel; **lo siento** I'm sorry
señal (f.) signal
señor (m.) Mr, gentleman
señora (f.) Mrs, lady, madam
señorita (f.) Miss, young lady
septiembre (m.) **setiembre**
 (m.) September
ser to be
servicio (m.) service; **los
 servicios** toilets
servir to serve
sesenta sixty
setecientos (as) seven hundred
setenta seventy
sevillano (a) Sevillian
sexo (m.) sex; **ambos sexos** both sexes
si if
sí yes
siempre always
siesta (f.) siesta; **dormir la siesta/echar
 una siesta** to have a siesta
siete seven
siglo (m.) century
significar to mean
siguiente following; **lo siguiente** the
 following
sin without
sitio (m.) place
sobre on; **sobre todo** above all
sol (m.) sun
solamente only
sólo only
solo (a) alone; **café solo** black coffee
soltero (a) bachelor, spinster
solucionar to resolve, solve
sombra (f.) shade, shadow
sombrero (m.) hat
sopa (f.) soup
su; **sus** his, hers, it's, one's, your, their
suave soft
subterráneo (m.) underground
subterráneo (a) underground
sucio (a) dirty
suelto (a) separate, loose
sumar to add
super (f.) 96 octane petrol
supuesto, **por supuesto** of course
sur (m.) south
suyo (a) his, hers, theirs, yours

tabaco (m.) tobacco
tal; **¿qué tal?** how are things?
talla (f.) size
tamaño (m.) size
también also
tampoco neither, nor
tanto as much, so much; **tanta gente** so
 many people
tapas (fp.) bar snacks
taquillero (a) ticket clerk
tardar en **¿cuánto tiempo tarda en
 llegar?** how long does it take to get
 there?
tarde late
tarde (f.) afternoon; **buenas tardes** good
 afternoon
tarjeta (f.) card
tarta helada ice-cream gâteau
taxista (m.) taxi driver
teatro (m.) theatre; **obra de teatro** play
Telefónica (f.) Telephone Company
teléfono (m.) telephone
televisar to televize
televisión (f.) television
temperatura (f.) temperature
templado (a) mild, lukewarm
temporada (f.) season **temporada
 alta** high season
temprano early
tendero (a) shopkeeper
tenedor (m.) fork
tener to have; **¿cuántos años tiene
 usted?** how old are you?; **tener que** to
 have to
tenis (m.) tennis
tercero (a) third; **tercera planta** third
 floor
terminación (f.) finish
terminar to finish
ternera (f.) veal; **ternera a la
 riojana** veal Riojan style
terraza (f.) terrace
tí you
tiempo (m.) time, weather
tienda (f.) shop; **ir de tiendas** to go
 shopping
tinto red (wine)
típico (a) typically Spanish
tipo (m.) type, kind
todo all; **sobre todo** above all; **todo
 seguido/todo recto** straight on
tomar to have, to take
tomate (m.) tomato
tono (m.) tone, shade
torero (m.) bullfighter
tormenta (f.) storm
torneo (m.) tournament
tortilla (f.) omelet **tortilla de patatas
 (f.)** potato omelet
total (m.) total
trabajar to work
trabajo (m.) work; job; **trabajo
 doméstico** housework
traer retraso to be late
traje (m.) outfit, suit
tranquilo (a) calm, quiet

traslado (m.) move, transfer
trece thirteen
treinta thirty
tren (m.) train
tres three
trescientos (as) three hundred
trucha (f.) trout
tu your
tú you
turismo (m.) tourism; la oficina de
  turismo (f.) tourist office
turista (m. and f.) tourist
turrón (m.) type of nougat made of
  almonds
tuyo (a) yours

último (a) last
un (a) one, a, an
uso (m.) use; uso normal normal usage
usted (Vd. Ud.) you
ustedes (Vds. Uds.) you (plural)
útil useful

vaca (f.) cow
vacación (f.) holiday
vainilla (f.) vanilla
valer to cost; ¿cuánto vale? how much
  is it?
vale OK, all right
valenciano (a) Valencian
valle (m.) valley
variación (f.) variation
variados (as) various; tapas
  variadas selection of tapas
variedad (f.) variety
varios(as) various, several
vaso (m.) glass
vecino (a) neighbour
vegetal vegetable aceite
  vegetal vegetable oil

veinte twenty
veinticinco twenty-five
vender to sell
venir to come
ver to see a ver let's see
verano (m.) summer
verdad (f.) truth; no es verdad it's not
  true
verde green
vertical vertical; los verticales clues
  down (crossword)
vestido (m.) dress
vestirse to get dressed
vez (f.) time; a veces at times; algunas
  veces sometimes en vez de instead
  of; más de una vez more than once
viajar to travel
viaje (m.) journey
viejo (a) old
viernes (m.) Friday
viento (m.) wind
vino (m.) wine
visitante (m.) visitor
visitar to visit
vivir to live
volver to come/go back
vosotros (as) you
vuelo (m.) flight

water (m.) lavatory

y and
ya now
yo I

zapato (m.) shoe
zoológico (m.) zoo
zumo(m.) juice

Index

Components/Just Listen 'n Learn Spanish	Code Number
Just Listen 'n Learn Spanish Course Book	7510-7
Cassette #1	7511-5
Cassette #2	7512-3
Cassette #3	7513-1

LANGUAGE AND TRAVEL BOOKS
FROM PASSPORT BOOKS

Dictionaries
Vox Spanish and English Dictionaries
Harrap's Concise Spanish and English
  Dictionary
Harrap French and English Dictionaries
Klett German and English Dictionary
Harrap's Concise German and English
  Dictionary
Everyday American English Dictionary
Beginner's Dictionary of American
  English Usage
Diccionario Inglés
El Diccionario del Español Chicano
Diccionario Básico Norteamericano
British/American Language Dictionary
The French Businessmate
The German Businessmate
The Spanish Businessmate
Harrap's Slang Dictionary (French and English)
English Picture Dictionary
French Picture Dictionary
Spanish Picture Dictionary
German Picture Dictionary

References
Guide to Spanish Idioms
Guide to German Idioms
Guide to Correspondence in Spanish
Guide to Correspondence in French
Español para los Hispanos
Business Russian
Yes! You Can Learn a Foreign Language
Everyday Japanese
Japanese in Plain English
Robin Hyman's Dictionary of Quotations
Passport's Japan Almanac

Verb References
Complete Handbook of Spanish Verbs
Spanish Verb Drills
French Verb Drills
German Verb Drills

Grammar References
Spanish Verbs and Essentials of Grammar
Nice 'n Easy Spanish Grammar
French Verbs and Essentials of Grammar
Nice 'n Easy French Grammar
German Verbs and Essentials of Grammar
Nice 'n Easy German Grammar
Italian Verbs and Essentials of Grammar
Essentials of Russian Grammar

Welcome Books
Welcome to Spain
Welcome to France
Welcome to Ancient Rome

**Just Listen 'n Learn Language
  Programs**
Complete language programs to learn
  Spanish, French, Italian, German and Greek.

Phrase Books
Just Enough Dutch
Just Enough French
Just Enough German
Just Enough Greek
Just Enough Italian
Just Enough Japanese
Just Enough Portuguese
Just Enough Scandinavian
Just Enough Serbo-Croat
Just Enough Spanish
Multilingual Phrase Book
International Traveler's Phrasebook

Language Game Books
Easy French Crossword Puzzles
Easy French Word Games and Puzzles
Easy Spanish Crossword Puzzles
Easy Spanish Word Games and Puzzles
Let's Learn About Series: Italy, France,
  Germany, Spain, America

Humor in Five Languages
The Insult Dictionary: How to Give 'Em
  Hell in 5 Nasty Languages
The Lover's Dictionary: How to Be
  Amorous in 5 Delectable Languages

Technical Dictionaries
Complete Multilingual Dictionary of
  Computer Terminology
Complete Multilingual Dictionary of
  Aviation and Aeronautical Terminology
Complete Multilingual Dictionary of
  Advertising, Marketing and Communications
Harrap's French and English
  Business Dictionary
Harrap's French and English
  Science Dictionary

Travel
Nagel's Encyclopedia Guides
World at Its Best Travel Series
Mystery Reader's Walking Guide: London
Japan Today
Bon Voyage!
Business Capitals of the World
Hiking and Walking Guide to Europe
European Atlas
Health Guide for International Travelers
Passport's Travel PAKS: Britain, Italy,
  France, Germany, Spain
Passport's China Guides

Getting Started Books
Introductory language books for Spanish,
  French, German and Italian.

PASSPORT BOOKS

Trade Imprint of National Textbook Company
4255 West Touhy Avenue
Lincolnwood, Illinois 60646-1975 U.S.A.